CONSUL IN PARADISE

SIXTY-EIGHT YEARS IN SIAM

CONSUL IN PARADISE

SIXTY-EIGHT YEARS IN SIAM

W. A. R. WOOD, C.M.G., C.I.E.

Former British Consul-General,
Chiengmai

SILKWORM BOOKS

ISBN 974-9575-12-1

First published in 1965 by
Souvenir Press, Ltd., London
and simultaneousely in Canada by
The Ryerson Press, Toronto
Reprinted in March 1968

This edition is published by Silkworm Books in 2003
For sale in Thailand only

Silkworm Books
104/5 Chiang Mai–Hot Road, M. 7, T. Suthep, Muang,
Chiang Mai 50200, Thailand
E-mail address: silkworm@loxinfo.co.th
Website: http://www.silkwormbooks.info

Typeset by Silk Type in Garamond 11 pt.
Cover photograph by Charansak Loimi
Printed in Thailand by O. S. Printing House, Bangkok

Contents

Illustrations

7617

We, Archibald Philip Earl of Rosebery, Viscount Rosebery, Viscount Inverkeithing, Baron Primrose and Dalmeny in the Peerage of Scotland; Baron Rosebery in the Peerage of the United Kingdom, a Baronet of Nova Scotia; a Member of Her Britannic Majesty's Most Honourable Privy Council; a Knight of the Most Noble Order of the Garter: Her Majesty's Principal Secretary of State for Foreign Affairs, &c. &c. &c.

Request and require in the Name of Her Majesty, all those whom it may concern to allow

William Alfred Rae Wood (British subject)

travelling on the Continent

to pass freely without let or hindrance, and to afford him every assistance and protection of which he may stand in need.

Given at the Foreign Office, London, the 6 day of September 1893

Rosebery

Signature of the Bearer.

W. A. R. Wood.

Author's original passport, 1893

Preface

This book, in a somewhat different form, was originally published in Bangkok, Siam, some time before World War II. During the war the premises of the press where it was printed were destroyed by a British bomb, and most of the copies of the book then in stock, as well as all the blocks for the illustrations, were lost.

The present edition contains four chapters not previously published, as well as a completely new set of illustrations.

If you are seeking for a serious review of Siamese history, politics, social customs, religion, folklore, or anything else, you will not find it in the following pages. This book contains, in fact, no information which is likely to be of practical use to anybody. It consists merely of a little of the froth collected by a cork which has floated for sixty-eight years on the seas of Siamese and Anglo-Siamese life. The cork, though by now a bit weather-beaten, is still floating, and still collecting froth.

I have throughout this book used the geographical name Siam. This is an English word to be found in all English dictionaries, and has been well known throughout the world for many hundreds of years. I prefer it, therefore, to the more modern name "Thailand". Similarly, when speaking or writing English, I would use the English geographical names Germany, Greece and Japan, though the people of those countries call them *Deutschland, Hellas* and *Nippon Koko* respectively.

Like most very old people, I tend to live in the past, and I like the old names and the old ways best. Even the modern flag of Siam, though the most attractive of the world's numerous tricolours, does not inspire in me the same affection as did the old white elephant flag. I should love to see that dear old flag flying once again before I die.

Readers who do not know Siam may perhaps be puzzled by my use of racial names. Let me therefore explain. The inhabitants of Siam, with unimportant exceptions, are all members of the Tai or Thai race. The people of the Kingdom of Laos, of the Shan States in Burma, and of a great part of Southern China, are also Tai or Thai, speaking languages or dialects which in all essential respects are the same as Siamese. The term *Siamese* is usually applied by foreigners to the Thai people of Southern or Central Siam. The inhabitants of Northern Siam, who speak a somewhat different dialect and until recently dressed rather differently, are referred to as *Laos.* This is seldom understood by visitors to Siam, who refer to everyone they meet as *Siamese,* thus falling into a similar error to that once committed by an intelligent French mayor. This gentleman was making a tour of Great Britain, and had learnt by heart a beautiful little pro-English speech, wherein he praised English men and women, scenery, literature, cookery and hospitality in very warm terms. He had worked off his speech with great success at civic functions given in his honour in London, Birmingham, Manchester and Newcastle, and when he was invited, at short notice, to Aberdeen, it never occurred to him that his oration needed any touching up, so he duly delivered it there too. To his surprise, it did not seem to go down very well, and on his nervously enquiring what was wrong, he was told that there was not a single Englishman in the room. For him, you see, every inhabitant of the United Kingdom was *Anglais,* just as for many visitors to Siam every Thai is Siamese.

If, therefore, readers of this book will try to think of places such as Chiengmai and Lampang, not as the Liverpool and Manchester of Siam, but rather as its Edinburgh and Aberdeen, they will find nothing to puzzle them.

Maybe one day the world will see a great Thai Empire, almost as big as China, uniting some 200,000 Thais under one flag—the white elephant, I hope—and all owing allegiance to one King; repeat KING.

It has been suggested to me that I should write something about the part played by Siam in World War II. I cannot bring myself to do this. I have long since forgiven the injuries which were inflicted on me during that painful period, and my only desire now is to forget them.

I must express my gratitude to Mr. Kraisri Nimman-haeminda, Mr. J. J. Boeles, and Mr. O. Gordon Young for their kind assistance, but for which it would have been impossible for me to write Chapter XIII on the Hill Tribes. Also to the Siam Society for their permission to publish photographs of which they own the copyright.

W.A.R.W.

Chiengmai,
January, 1965.

I

Old Days in Bangkok

I arrived in Bangkok as a Student Interpreter in July 1896. I was just eighteen-and-a-half years old—the youngest Consular Officer who ever came to Siam, or, I think, to any other eastern post.

There were two of us, M. being a couple of years my senior. We were paid £200 a year and were provided with an unfurnished house. The first day we landed, we were presented with a bill for furniture, amounting to £75. I cannot remember how we managed to pay it, for we had no money—but I *do* remember the furniture.

The office of Student Interpreter originated, I believe, in the Levant, and originally a Student Interpreter was a person who studied to become an Interpreter. Interpreters, I think, at one time existed in China, but long ago became merged into the ordinary Consular service. In Siam such posts never existed, so that a Student Interpreter was, in effect, a probationer Vice-Consul. The one thing he never had to do was to interpret Siamese. I was occasionally asked to interpret in the Consular Court, but the languages for which I was needed were French and German, never Siamese.

In theory, we were supposed to devote most of our time for the first two years to the study of the Siamese language. In practice, we were told that we could have the afternoons off, but must work in the Consular office for three mornings a week each, turn about. After about a week of this, it was found that the valuable services of both of us were required every morning, and a month or so later we were wanted in the afternoon as well. So we learnt Siamese when we could find the time. We had two teachers, one of whom knew some English, the other not. Neither of them had any idea of teaching, so we had to set our own lessons. I cannot think how either of us managed to learn anything at all, but in fact we both did pretty well. At the end of the two years we could speak, read and write Siamese more or less, and passed our examination with flying colours, M. beating me by five marks. Siamese writing was, I may say, an accomplishment only attained by one of our predecessors.

We had to do all sorts of office work. M. was factotum to the Consular Court, whilst I helped with the accounts and shipping, besides acting as typist and secretary to the Minister. I was the first typist the Legation ever had, and a pretty bad one, too; but the Minister was delighted with this rare accomplishment of mine.

Shipping duties were quite onerous in those early days, as most of the steamers plying between Bangkok and Singapore or Hongkong were British, though a few years later they were almost all sold to the Norddeutscher Lloyd Company. There were also a few sailing vessels calling from time to time, and when one of these was in port, I was usually kept busy with disputes between the Captain and crew.

When I look back, I find it astounding that I, a mere boy, and young for my years, ever managed to exercise any sort of control over a lot of tough old salts, or to coerce gentlemen of the type of Captain Kettle, especially when they were drunk, as was often the case. But I did it somehow. At first I worked under C., about four years my senior, and I learnt a lot from him, though I never managed to become quite so autocratic as he was. He had a wonderful faculty for handling tough cases.

I recollect a case in which some of the crewmen of a certain ship had banded together to murder the Captain. They had had two tries before the ship reached Bangkok, and when she arrived half the crew were in irons, and the Captain was swathed up in yards of bandages. He wanted to sign off the entire crew, but we refused to let him, fearing to have them destitute on our hands. My job was to track down exactly which of the men were in the plot. After almost endless enquiries I succeeded, and the guilty ones were duly jailed by the Consular Court. To take their place, three Chinese and one young Siamese were brought along. I felt sorry for the Siamese, a lad of about my own age, named Kham, whose only experience of the sea was on a fishing boat. I took him aside, and begged him not to go to sea with that tough gang, unable, as he was, even to make himself understood by them. But he had the spirit of adventure in him, and off he went, though I remember that he shed a few tears.

Years later we were asked by the Board of Trade in London to try to trace Kham's relations, as he had died in Liverpool. It so happened that I had made a note of the address of his parents, and I went myself to tell them that their son was dead. He had saved quite a lot of money, which was sent to them in due course. I do not think they worried much, for they had a large family, and had almost forgotten poor Kham.

Sailors used to die in Bangkok of every kind of disease except sunstroke. As they were wont to wander around in the hottest sun, clad in thick woollen suits—often, too, full of the most poisonous liquor—I never understood how they escaped sunstroke; but they did somehow.

Now and then a sailor who could not swim would fall into the river and be drowned. Sometimes the corpse was never found. Once a dead seaman was left by the tide on the Legation landing, and I was called upon to help to get him out and put him in a coffin. I have done a lot of undertaking in my time, but that was about my worst job. The poor fellow had been in the river for about a week, and his arms were stretched out perfectly straight and stiff. How we managed to stuff him into the coffin I really do not know, but I remember that I took a good many whiskies both before and after the operation.

Undertaking was all in the day's work. There was a German undertaker in Bangkok, rather rough and ready in his methods, and one of us Consular lads had to superintend him, see that his coffins fitted, and that all incidental arrangements were in order. A clergyman had often to be found at short notice. This was usually easy, as in addition to an elderly English parson, there were several American Presbyterian missionaries in Bangkok; but now and then some hitch would occur, and then M, or I had to read the Burial Service. M. did it much better than I, which he attributed to the fact that his father was a clergyman. On one occasion the widow of a dead man absolutely refused to let me read the service, saying that I was too young, so I had to go back home and bring M. to do it. Even then she was not satisfied, and told him that he mumbled. Some people are impossible to please.

Another time the mother of a little child which we were burying specially asked me to read part of the service, though we had a clergyman there, on the ground that I was young and innocent. Of course I did as she wished, and I remember that I was very much affected, though, alas! I was hardly so innocent as she thought me, even in those distant days.

When I first came to Bangkok, the months of March, April and May were usually known as the *cholera season*. There was no water supply in the town then, and the poorer classes had to drink the water of the Menam River or of one of the numerous canals which intersected the city and its suburbs. We foreigners used to store up rain water in jars, and were very nervous about drinking any water the origin of which we did not know. No reliable death register was kept, but in bad years the number of deaths from cholera must have been enormous. The Chinese were the chief victims. People brought up in Bangkok, and accustomed to drinking river water from the day of their birth, probably acquired some degree of immunity against cholera germs, but the Chinese possessed no such immunity, and having no other water to drink except that from the river or the canals, they used to die like flies. Driving along the New Road, as the central thoroughfare of Bangkok was—and is—called, one sometimes passed whole rows of Chinese coffins being borne along. As for Europeans, deaths among them were quite frequent, in spite of all the precautions they took. At the United Club one would ask in the evening: "Where is Jones?" and be told he was dead of cholera. "And Brown?" "Dead too." "And Robinson?" "Laid up with cholera."

How people caught cholera nobody ever really knew. One man of my acquaintance drank nothing but soda-water imported from Singapore, had all the water used in his kitchen boiled in his presence, and personally dipped all his plates and cutlery into boiling water before using. Yet one night he was suddenly seized with cholera, and died in a few hours.

When the prisoners in the Consular jail were attacked by cholera, as happened now and then, M. and I were sometimes called up in the night to help to deal with them. I remember one warder and three convicts all being taken ill in one night. The warder was sick all over me, and though the doctor assured me that there was no special danger in this, somehow or other I did not like it at all, and scrubbed myself all over with Jeyes fluid when I got home.

Though I utterly despise people, whether in the West or the East, who go about in terror of being infected with some disease, I will admit that I have a sort of dislike of cholera. When it is prevalent, one is forced to regard with distrust everything one eats or drinks, which removes all pleasure from life. Moreover, the spectacle of a cholera patient is very distressing. I remember one of our servants, a fellow of about twenty, who was taken ill with cholera early one morning. When I was called in to see him at about 9 a.m. he looked like a man of eighty, with blue, sunken face, and sagging flesh. This man was cured by injecting salt water into his veins, and recovered almost as suddenly as he had been taken ill. It was like seeing a corpse come to life before one's eyes.

Cholera, thank God, is very rare in Bangkok now, owing to the excellent water supply installed by the Siamese Government, but it makes its appearance now and then in other parts of Siam.

As for bubonic plague, it does not worry me much. Of course, I would rather not catch it, but somehow the probability of such a thing occurring seems much more remote than in the case of cholera. The first *official* outbreak of bubonic plague in Siam was in 1902, but it must almost certainly have occurred before, though not correctly diagnosed. Plague has been endemic in Southern China from time immemorial, and there has always been a trade between Siam and China with junks and other sailing-ships. As no sanitary or quarantine precautions were taken until comparatively recent times, it is absurd to suppose that infection was never carried in all that long period. When European doctors first diagnosed bubonic plague in 1902, some of my Siamese friends told me that the disease was well known to them under the name of "khai phit", and that they had seen numerous cases.

However this may be, the first *official* cases of bubonic plague were supposed to be due to infection from fleas carried in bales of rugs from India. These were opened in a place called Tük Khao, which is a settlement of Indian Mahomedans, or Pakistanis, as we must call them now. At that time, Tük Khao was almost like a little city in itself, and quite easily isolated, but when the first deaths from plague occurred there the inhabitants were most reluctant to submit to the restrictions imposed by the Public Health authorities, and kept on creeping out at night, saying that they could not obtain sufficient food. The British Minister sent me up to deal with them, and I spent many days there, organising their food arrangements and using my influence to make them observe the quarantine rules, and submit to the burning of a number of huts and sheds, as well as to the disinfection of their houses. At first I felt a bit uncomfortable when I had to go into rooms where plague patients were lying dead, but I got over that foolish feeling by the end of the first day. The Indians liked having me there, and openly said that if I went away they would refuse to submit to any sort of coercion, even if they were shot. So I had to go there every day and all day, until no more cases occurred.

Before any human beings were attacked by plague at Tük Khao, a number of rats died, as is usual, and also a large number of pigeons, which I have not heard of elsewhere; but it may have been only a coincidence.

Any rats we caught were cremated. I recollect the Chief Medical Officer telling a Malay policeman to burn two rats. He used the word for *cook* instead of *burn*, and the policeman fried the two rats in ghee, and brought them along tastefully served up on a plate, evidently thinking that we wanted to eat them. The Medical Officer was furious, and could not see how funny it was.

Smallpox used to be very common in Siam, and still occurs now and then in districts where people have neglected to be vaccinated. I have looked after a lot of smallpox patients, and have vaccinated hundreds of people, using a darning needle. It is astounding how nervous many people are about being vaccinated, even with a darning needle. I have known a stalwart Englishman to turn pale with fear when I brandished my needle at him. I always jabbed nervous people extra deep with the needle.

Siam provides a complete disproof of one of the principal arguments of the anti-vaccinationists. This is to the effect that the decrease of smallpox in Europe is not due to vaccination, but to improved sanitation and cleaner habits, the introduction of which was more or less contemporaneous with the discovery of vaccination. But in Siam vaccination was introduced long before there was any improvement in sanitation, yet as soon as people began to be vaccinated smallpox decreased enormously, though in every other matter which might encourage infection conditions for longremained exactly as they had been for hundreds of years back.

Nobody in Siam argues about the efficacy of vaccination. It is a patent and evident fact. So ready, indeed, are most people to be vaccinated that they are sometimes exploited by quacks and swindlers. During one smallpox scare a bogus doctor vaccinated the entire population of three villages with Nestle's condensed milk at five cents a head.

Leprosy is often met with in Siam, and there is no law compelling the segregation of lepers, though there are several voluntary asylums.

Leprosy is not a very contagious disease. It is possible to live for years and years among lepers and never catch it, and the chances of acquiring it by casual contact are negligible.

When I was first in Bangkok there were several lepers, some without toes or fingers, rowing public ferry boats on the Menam River, and nobody worried about any danger of infection. One was expected to give them a tip in addition to the usual fare.

Many lepers in Siam do not care to enter the excellent asylums which have been provided for them, either by the Government, or by charitable people, both Siamese and foreign. They do not like the few restrictions under which they must necessarily be placed in an institution, and prefer to wander about begging.

In the island of Koh-si-chang in the Gulf of Siam, where we used to go for a holiday now and then, there was a family of lepers, consisting of an old woman, her daughter and her little grandson. They lived in a ramshackle hut, and the old woman used to sit in the doorway and croon a sort of dirge about her troubles. The first time I was there the daughter died, and M. and I were paid to bury her; we also offered to repair the hut, but the old woman refused, saying: "My daughter is gone, and I am almost gone, and the little boy will not last much longer." The next year I went there again, and found that the poor little lad had just died, but the old dame still sat there crooning away. The hut was so wobbly that it seemed ready to collapse any minute, but still she refused to have it repaired. The third year I found the hut lying in ruins, and the old woman was there no more. The village people told me she had died only a week before, and the little hut collapsed when they were carrying her away to bury.

I wonder whether all Consular Officers dislike Distressed British Subjects (generally called D.B.Ss.) as much as I did. Of course, there are genuine D.B.Ss., and the duty of helping these is one which is a pleasure to perform. What I call a genuine D.B.S. is a person residing in the Consular Officer's district who has had the misfortune to become destitute. The Foreign Office permits a Consul to help such people to return home, and most Consuls are glad to add a bit out of their own pockets to what is strictly necessary. But cases like this are rare. The usual sort of D.B.S. is a beachcomber, who begs, borrows or steals enough money to get from one foreign port to the next, and then applies to the local Consul to feed, house and clothe him, and finally to send him on to repeat the performance somewhere else. The Foreign Office is extremely sticky about refunding advances made to such gentry; and rightly so, for why should the heavily burdened British taxpayer be forced to meet the travelling expenses of his unworthy brethren? On the other hand, what is an unfortunate Consul to do when a British subject, often an educated man, strolls in and says, in effect: Here I am, penniless. House me, or I'll sleep in the street. Feed me, or I'll die on your doorstep. And send me away, or you'll have to house and feed me forever!

I wonder how many hundreds of people there are who travel all over the world gratis. They have to swallow a lot of insults and put up with a good deal of discomfort, but they soon get used to that, and go on travelling for years on end, with all their expenses paid by their Consuls or by their charitable fellow countrymen.

Of course, the Consul has to send them on in the end, and the quicker he does it the cheaper it comes in the long run.

In the old days, when we had a Consular Court, the D.B.S.

difficulty was often met by handing the D.B.S. a couple of ticals and telling him to call again the next day. He would then go out and get tight, and would probably bash some-body—with luck a policeman—on the head. The Siam Order in Council permitted the Consular Court to deport to British territory any British subject found guilty of a criminal offence. So the D.B.S. would be hauled up before the Court, charged with assault or disorderly conduct, sentenced to a short term of imprisonment, and promptly shipped to Singapore.

Quite a number of D.B.S.s used to walk across from Burma, over a week's march through the jungle, and were very hurt and disgusted if it was suggested that they should walk back again—really a most reasonable idea.

D.B.S.s are always "looking for work", even in distant villages in the interior, where it is clear that there are no possible jobs for Europeans.

When it comes to a question of paying a railway fare for them, D.B.S.s invariably contend that it is derogatory to British prestige to send them third class, and demand at least a second class ticket.

I have had D.B.S.s walk boldly up to my house, complete with suitcase, proposing to stay there. I even once found one fast asleep on my bed, full of my whisky.

One D.B.S. told me that he was a vaudeville artiste, and claimed that he could earn enough to pay his expenses away if he could get hold of a hall and an audience. This was not in Bangkok, but at Chiengmai, and as the expense of getting rid of undesirables from that post is particularly heavy, I actually hired a hall for him, and persuaded two storekeepers to exhibit handbills and sell tickets for his performance. Quite a big audience assembled, but when the critical moment came, the artiste was too tight to appear; so I had to refund the ticket money, pay for the hall, and send the artiste away by public subscription.

Another D.B.S. said he was a conjuror, and I accordingly assisted him to give a performance, undeterred by my bad experience with the vaudeville artiste. In his first trick he had to fire off a pistol, but being rather pickled, he put in a loaded cartridge in mistake for a blank one, and shot himself in the leg. So the show broke up, and I had to pay his doctor's bill as well as his fare. In this case, I refused to consider any question of refunding the ticket money as I thought it well worth paying a small sum to see a D.B.S. shoot himself even though only in the leg.

One day some wretched Consul, goaded to desperation, will strangle a D.B.S. When this happens, I shall be glad to make a generous donation towards the cost of his defence.

In my early days in Bangkok, I was a sort of general factotum at garden parties and other social functions at the Legation. Queen Victoria's birthday was the occasion of an annual garden party, which brought together a large assembly of all races. M and I helped to unload royal and distinguished guests from their carriages, and passed them along to be received by the Minister and his wife. Before the second garden party of my time, the Minister said to me:

"Wood, last year two men came here drunk, and made perfect nuisances of themselves. If anyone arrives here tight this year, please try to shunt them off." I promised to do my best, and arranged to have an empty gharry waiting not far from the place where Mr. and Mrs. Minister received their guests. If M. spotted a drunk on the side where he was unloading guests, he was to signal to me by blowing his nose with a red silk handkerchief. Ere long, I unloaded a very mellow guest. I took him quickly to the Minister and Mrs. Z., let him shake hands with them, and then led him straight to the gharry, bade him goodbye, shoved him in, and told the syce to drive away before he really quite knew what was happening. At the same moment I observed M. frantically blowing his nose with the red silk handkerchief. We were not prepared for two cases in such quick succession. However, I felt that something must be done, so I hurried along, took charge of M's drunk, presented him hurriedly to his host andhostess, and then led him to the place where the hired gharries were standing. Hailing a syce whom I knew, I tried to put the unwelcome guest into his gharry, but he refused to get in, saying that he had only just arrived. "But everybody is leaving, old chap," said I; "I am leaving myself, and want you to give me a lift." "What!" said he, "drive with you wearing no hat. Shernly not. It ishn't respectable." Such was the social code of those days.

Hastily borrowing a peaked cap from another syce, I put my handkerchief on my head, perched the cap, four sizes too small, on top of it, dragged my bibulous friend into the gharry, and drove with him to the Oriental Hotel; there I left him propped against the bar, drinking Queen Victoria's health with a few congenial spirits. I never found out who he was.

There was a British gunboat in port at the time, and as I was wearing a double-breasted blue serge suit, I hoped that, with the syce's cap, I might be taken for a naval officer. But I do not think I was.

When a gunboat came to Bangkok, we generally gave the officers a very good time, as well as providing entertainments for the crew. We had many naval visitors who later became famous, Earl Jellicoe among them.

A tragic fate befell a young bluejacket who undertook to paint the Legation flagstaff for us. This is one of the highest Legation flagstaffs in the world, and was then popularly supposed to be the abode of an evil spirit. We had been accustomed, when the flagstaff needed painting, to hire a Malay for the job. Before starting work, a day was always set aside for the presentation of offerings to propitiate the spirit, such things as beef, fruit and flowers being placed at the base of the flagstaff, and candles and incense burnt.

The young sailor I mentioned, hearing that the flagstaff was to be painted, volunteered for the job. His Captain gave him leave to take it on, and to accept a fee equal to the sum we used to pay the Malay. Of course, to a bluejacket the ascent was mere child's play, and he thought nothing of it at all. Our Siamese servants expressed anxiety about the business,

as the spirit had not been propitiated, but we paid no attention
to this; still less did the sailor.

When the poor fellow had fixed up his tackle and was just
starting to paint the upper half of the flagstaff, he suddenly
threw up his arms and fell with fearful force on the ground; he
was terrible injured, and died in a few seconds. We thought
that perhaps he had been affected by the sun, but of course
the general opinion was that the spirit was responsible.

Besides British, we often had foreign men-of-war in Bangkok. One of my earliest recollections is the genial figure of the
Captain of the Russian gunboat *Askold*, later sunk in the
Russo-Japanese war. This old sea-dog used to stand in the bar
of the United Club, ordering drinks all round and would
introduce himself to strangers in these terms: "My name is
Pantzoff. I am here wid der *Askold*. But I have der varm heart."

There used to be a very large number of thieves and burglars
in Bangkok. Even at the present time there are a good number.
I must have been burgled at least a dozen times. A favourite
method of thieves was to watch a house in the evening until
the dining-room punkah was seen moving. This meant that
masters and servants were all busy for at least half an hour
with the great function of dinner, and that the entire upper
floor of the house was free for an uninterrupted burglary. A
man would then climb up the verandah, remove any loose
valuables he could find, tie them in a bundle, and throw them
down to his pal.

I once woke up in the night, and hearing a noise, struck a
match. A burglar was standing quite close to me in the
verandah. When he saw me he jumped, without the slightest
hesitation, clean out of the verandah window, which was at
least twenty-five feet from the ground. I raised the alarm, and
went down to look at the corpse, but there was no trace of the
burglar except a crushed hibiscus bush on which he had
landed.

We had, of course, watchmen, but I do not think they ever
prevented a burglary or caught a thief. They were Indians,

there being a sort of superstition throughout Siam that all watchmen ought to be Indians. I cannot think why. Some say that it is because they are big and strong, but people are quite ready to employ small and feeble watchmen, provided they are Indians.

The manager of a French firm once complained to me that his Indian watchman had opened his safe with a false key, stolen a large sum of money, and disappeared. He seemed to think that I was partly to blame, because the man was a British subject. I asked where the man had been engaged, and found that the Frenchman had met him by accident, when travelling in the forest north of the town of Nan, and had instantly engaged him on a good salary. On making enquiries at Nan, I found that the man in question had, when he met his new employer, just been released from the local jail, where he had been serving a long term of imprisonment for burglary and attempted murder.

My French friend thought that he had acted quite reasonably in engaging the man, as the latter held a British registration certificate, was very tall, and had a long black beard. I think it was really the beard which decided him. Personally, I considered that he was lucky not to have had his throat cut in addition to losing his money.

C. once gave his Chinese servant a pair of shoes to take to be mended. Just after dinner that night, a fearful row was heard outside the office. We ran out, and found poor Ah Yong in the grip of one of our Indian watchmen. The latter was very loath to release his captive, and nothing would persuade him that he had not collared a dangerous shoe burglar.

A week later we were cleared out by real burglars. The watchman, on being interrogated the next morning, said that he had seen a man slinking out of our house at 2 a.m., carrying a bundle. "Why the........ didn't you catch him?" "Well, you see, last week I caught a shoe burglar, and you told me I was wrong, and forced me to let him go."

Fires used constantly to occur in Bangkok. Even now, they are not uncommon, and in my early days they were always breaking out. There were whole quarters of the town built of timber, and thousands of houses with attap thatch roofs. The speed with which fires spread was appalling, and it was a most pitiful sight to see poor people escaping along the narrow lanes, carrying as much of their modest property as they had time to snatch up in their hasty flight. All the thieves in Bangkok would flock to a fire, and, while pretending to help to save people's goods, would bolt with whatever they could get hold of. Luckily few lives were ever lost, as most of the buildings were low, and even upper storeys were not difficult to escape from.

The scene of a fire on the following day was very distressing. An area of black, smouldering ashes, hundreds of charred stumps of house posts, and crowds of poor, destitute people, poking about among the ruins of their vanished homes, vainly hoping to unearth a few of their little treasures. Rarely did they find anything. What the flames had spared, the thieves had plundered.

One of our annual social events in Bangkok was a Chinese dinner, given by the Fish Farmer, who happened to be a British subject. The Fish Farmer was a man who, in return for an annual payment, was empowered by the Siamese Government to collect and keep all taxes on the fisheries in the Menam River. Many other taxes were at that time farmed out in the same way. The Fish Farmer always had a supply of magnificent fish at his place, and often made us presents of some of it. His Chinese dinners were sumptuous affairs. I do not know how many courses there were—there seemed to be hundreds—and everything was washed down by fine old cognac.

Fish, within reason, from the Fish Farmer, was understood to be a present which a British Consular Officer could legitimately accept. The whole question of accepting presents is a difficult one. In India, I believe, definite regulations used to be laid down for the guidance of civil servants, but Consular Officers have to rely on their own discretion in this matter. In Siam it is a usual and customary thing for a man calling on a person of superior position to take a little present with him. This need not be of any great intrinsic value. A few oranges or bananas, a bunch of flowers or a home-made cake will do very well, and to refuse to accept such little gifts would be thought both churlish and unkind. There is no analogy whatever between such little goodwill offerings and things, for instance, like a large eighteen carat gold chronometer, which a Chinese litigant once tried to get me to accept.

One of my colleagues was so terrified of acquiring a Baconian reputation that he always refused even the tiniest gifts, thus gaining, I fear, instead of the respect which he coveted, merely the name of being harsh and ill-mannered. A Chinese visitor once called on him, and not finding him at home, left two melons and a small bunch of roses at his house. On his return he nearly had a fit, and hurriedly despatched an office messenger by boat to take the offending articles back. I happened to be seated on the river-landing with the Minister, and we enquired of the man where he was going. On hearing of the circumstances, the Minister was horribly indignant. "Great Heavens!" cried he, "what a stinking reputation the Consular service in Siam must have, if X. fears to be suspected of perverting justice for the sake of two stale melons and a bunch of faded roses!"

When a Consul visited a country town or village, it was usual for the British subjects there to bring him a few flowers or some home-grown fruit. In places where sugar-cane was grown, they often brought a few sticks of cane. The actual value of each gift of cane is practically nil, but I have often been greatly embarrassed by the aggregate amount brought, yet realising that it would seem ungracious to refuse it, and rude to leave it behind.

Shan and Burmese British subjects had a simple, natural kind of courtesy inherent in their natures, and thoroughly understood the proper etiquette of giving presents, but some British subjects belonging to other races did not always show the same tact. They often insisted on buying presents of canned provisions, beer, whisky, or even more expensive articles. When a storekeeper brought along a couple of cans of condensed milk from his store, no great harm was done, but when a man purchased provisions worth several pounds, it was very unpleasant. A Consul cannot accept such presents, but in refusing them he has to be polite, and avoid seeming in any way annoyed, as the donor means no harm. On the other hand, the mere fact of the things being refused is bound to upset their owner, for he cannot take them away again without looking awkward, and appearing to have suffered a rebuff from the Consul.

In a certain town which I once visited, some of the local residents, with the kindest intentions, bought up most of the canned provisions and alcoholic drinks in the place, and brought them to me on a gaily decorated lorry, with a brass band on another lorry in front, playing the Dead March in *Saul*. The extreme publicity of this presentation made it so much the more painful for all concerned when the lorries, laden as before, had to go back again. Next day the band came round and complained that they had not been paid, and I had to coerce my would-be benefactors into paying the band for tooting the Dead March over the gifts which I had turned down.

It was all very painful, and very unnecessary, for the proper etiquette of gifts is, as I said above, quite easy to observe.

There were, in my early days, an enormous number of pawn-shops in Bangkok. They were all owned by Chinese, many of the pawnbrokers being British or French subjects, and a good number of Macao Portuguese Chinese. There were then no pawnshop regulations, and many—I fear most—of the pawn-brokers were little better than fences, ready to take anything in pawn, no matter how suspicious the circumstances. When one was burgled, one waited a bit, and then went round the pawnshops, where the stolen property would quite likely be seen exposed for sale. I had two or three Chinese friends in the business, and was usually able to get back my own and my foreign friends' stolen property on favourable terms; but the ordinary victim had the choice between losing his valuables, or buying them back on the pawn-broker's terms.

The pawnbrokers' shops in Bangkok were, and still are, most interesting, containing all sorts of valuable articles, such as jewellery, gold and silverware, porcelain, silk, etc.

Pawnshops are now under very strict regulations, and if a pawnbroker wants to act as a fence he has to do it on the quiet, and not in the open manner in which he carried on the business sixty years ago.

I once had a valuable silver vase stolen, which I met with later in a pawnshop. I knew quite well who was the thief, and that he was a person whom the pawnbroker could not possibly have believed to be the owner of the vase, so I uttered some rather caustic remarks on the subject. The pawnbroker appeared to be very contrite, and begged me to accept the vase without payment. As it was my own, and as I looked upon the pawnbroker as an accessory to the theft, I took it. A few days later, the pawnbroker came to the Consulate and asked me to register him as a British subject. He had no evidence whatever to show that he really was a British subject, but he clearly thought that he had placed me under such an obligation by giving me back my own vase, that I could not decently refuse his request. So I had to pay him a good sum for the vase, which he accepted very unwillingly, evidently thinking me a very slippery customer.

In those days many people, especially Chinese, were very desirous of obtaining British registration certificates, the possession of which secured for them exemption from certain taxes, as well as other privileges—for instance, their premises could not be searched by the police without a warrant from the British Consular Court. One of the Consular clerks once reported to me that he had been offered a bribe of a thousand ticals to assist in obtaining a registration certificate for a certain Chinese merchant, and all sorts of tricks were resorted to in order to induce unwary Consular Officers to issue registration certificates to persons not really entitled to them.

I will give one example. A hard-up old Chinese British subject had a son, aged about nineteen, who paid a visit to
Hongkong and died there. A wealthy young Chinaman, hearing this, bribed the father to let him impersonate the dead
youth, to introduce him to the Consul as his son, and to obtain a registration certificate for him. This was done, the certificate was duly issued by the unsuspecting Consul, and all
would have gone well but for the fact that the dead son had,
without the knowledge of his parents, married a Siamese girl.
The young widow was expecting a baby, and went to her fa-
ther-in-law to ask for money. He, knowing nothing about her,
put her off, whereupon she went straight to complain to the
British Consul. During the investigation of her claim the
whole fraud came to light.

In other similar cases it is probable that we were often
imposed upon with more permanent success.

Sport in Bangkok at the end of last century was a good deal
more happy-go-lucky than it is now. Races were held as a rule
only once a year, on the Pramane ground, a large public
space near the Royal Palace. Only Siamese ponies were
raced, and many of the jockeys were amateurs. I myself once
rode in a race on a small Siamese pony of some fame called
Pailin, and came in third. I am sure that I should have fallen
off, but for the fact that I steadied myself now and then by
touching the ground on either side with one or other of my
feet.

It did not cost much to keep racing ponies. In fact, I started
a racing stable myself, though my pay was only £200 a year.
My stable contained only one pony, named Chao Phya. It cost
me £10, and unfortunately it died of *surra* before making its
debut on the course. So I gave up my racing stable, as I could
not raise £10 to buy another pony.

A few enthusiasts used to try to get up cricket on Sunday
mornings, also on the Pramane ground, but they never got
much encouragement. For good players, cricket may perhaps
provide some exercise and amusement. For poor players like
myself it provides neither. One stands at the wicket for about

two minutes, someone yells "Out", and one is then permitted
to sit for hours, or maybe days, watching other people play;
after this fatiguing experience, one is set on to the job of
fielding, which is the sort of thing I prefer to pay little boys to
do for me.

As for golf, it is worse than cricket, for the better a man plays
the less exercise he gets. In the old days, we used to play golf
on the Pramane ground, and as there were always large numbers of people walking about, not to mention troops drilling,
it was quite a ticklish affair. Nobody ever yelled "Fore", because it was always "Fore" all the time, and nobody would have
paid any attention, anyhow. It came to be understood that you
were allowed to hit ordinary members of the public on any
part of the body for nothing, but that you must pay them one
tical if you hit them on the head or face. To hit priests came a
good bit more expensive, and of course if you were so unlucky
as to hit a person of high rank, anything might happen. Why
anyone ever wanted to play golf on the Pramane ground is a
mystery to me; but golfers would rather play anywhere than
nowhere, which only shows what unreasonable people they
are.

I know a lot about golf, having played it since 1885, and
when I am too decrepit to walk I shall take it up seriously.
There used to be an old gentleman in Bangkok who did this.
He was so infirm that he not only could not walk, but was
unable to stand without assistance, so he rightly decided that
golf was just the game for him. He used to be wheeled in a
rickshaw to the first tee; his servant then helped him out and
held him up while he drove off; he was then put back into the
rickshaw and dragged away after the ball. He soon became very
expert, and defeated many stalwart young golfing athletes.

I spoke above of the Fish Farmer. There were several much
more important tax farmers in Bangkok, the two biggest being
the Opium and the Gambling Farmers. The Gambling Farmer
ran a number of gambling houses in different parts of Bangkok, and one of the entertainments for globe-trotters was to

The author when he looked young and innocent.

The author's wife, aged 22 years.

Chiengmai Consular elephants starting on a journey, 1915.
The elephant to the extreme left is the one which dug up and ate corpses.

King Prachathipok entering Chiengmai on elephant back, 1926.
There were eighty-four elephants in the procession.

The execution, *c.* 1903. This is not the execution described in the text.

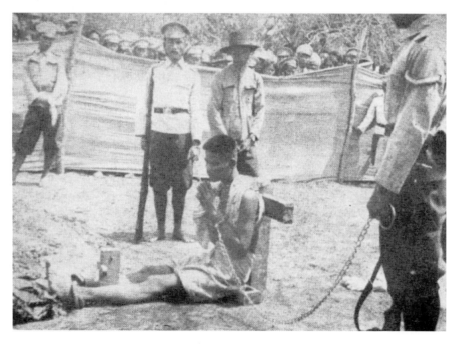

take them round to see a gambling house. All sorts of games of chance were played, but the most popular was fantan, called *Tua* by the Siamese. This very simple game has been described hundreds of times, so I will only say briefly that it consists in the banker taking at random a number of cowrie shells and counting them out in heaps of four; the players stake on the number of shells which they expect will be in the last heap, that is to say on the numbers one, two, three or four, or on certain combinations of these. In Bangkok they used to count out about half the shells in heaps of five, then pause, and count out the remainder in heaps of four. After the pause, no further bets were accepted.

M. and I got hold of a book on gambling systems, which we were persuaded was almost infallible. Unfortunately, we could not try it out often enough for a real test, as we were afraid of getting a bad name. We tried to do a round of all the different gambling houses, numbering about twelve, but soon found that there were several frightful looking ruffians doing the same, and when they started greeting us as old pals, we had to give up our attempt to find the perfect system. One thing we did prove to our own satisfaction, namely that if one waited till the last possible moment to lay down one's stake, and then staked on the number most favourable to the banker, one was likely to win. This seems reasonable. A very moderately skilled conjuror can get rid of pigeons, rabbits, watches, and all kinds of comparatively bulky objects, and a Chinese fantan banker who could not manage to spirit away one or two cowrie shells would be a pretty poor sort of bungler.

The abolition of public gambling houses by King Chulalongkorn was one of the wisest measures of that excellent monarch, for the gambling houses were centres of every sort of crime and wickedness. There were plenty of young fellows who spent their whole lives around the gambling houses, sleeping in some nearby hut, and eating at one of the adjoining food stalls. One or two of them told me quite frankly that they had never done anything but gamble. If they had no money they went out and stole something, or often they would beg for a little money from some specially lucky gambler, who was always ready to oblige them.

The astonishing thing about these professional gamblers was the badness of their play. Of course fantan—the question of cheating being disregarded—is a game of pure chance; but even in a game of chance there are some sorts of foolishness which greatly increase the chances of losing.

The typical gambling-house loafer, known as a *nakleng,* affected a particular type of costume. He usually wore a gaily coloured silk *sarong,* a shirt of very thin flowered muslin, and a huge imitation Panama hat, known as a pineapple fibre hat. It was the recognised uniform of ruffianism.

A striking thing about the Bangkok gambling houses was the good temper of the crowd, which, after all, was largely composed of the dregs of society. With an English or American crowd, I am sure, there would have been a row every few minutes, and now and then some extra tough customer would have smashed the place up. But in Bangkok everything went very smoothly. If you won, you won; if you lost, you lost, and that was the end of it. Once or twice I saw somebody get a little bit quarrelsome and talkative; when this happened, the offender, by some almost imperceptible means, found himself in a few seconds outside in the street; and he came back no more that night.

The extent to which people gambled was shown by the coinage. A silver tical, being a thick and heavy coin, could easily be scooped in by a fantan banker with his bamboo rake, but small silver coins, being much thinner, were apt to slip under the edge, thus wasting valuable time. Small coins were therefore invariably punched into a sort of bunch or lump for gambling purposes. With the exception of pieces fresh from the mint, such a thing as an unpunched silver coin did not exist in Siam.

The so-called bullet ticals were still in use when I first came to Siam, though they had not been minted since about 1860. They were shaped like a somewhat oblong bullet, with the ends pinched inwards, and were very inconvenient to count or to carry about, and very easy to counterfeit. Only an expert could detect a bad bullet tical. One could test them by scratching them, but a scratched tical was quite useless, for the scratching was looked upon as a certificate of suspiciousness, and nobody would risk taking it thereafter.

Both the bullet and the flat ticals were heavy and cumbrous coins to carry about, though less so than silver dollars. Still, there is a good deal to be said in favour of money which does not go up in smoke if your house catches fire, or turn into jelly when you happen to fall into a ditch.

II

British Courts in Siam

The British Court in Siam began to function after the conclusion of the Treaty of 1855, which granted extra-territorial rights to Great Britain. It continued as a *Consular* Court until the year 1902. In that year, under the aegis of a Consul with legal qualifications, it blossomed forth into His Britannic Majesty's Court for Siam, with at first one and later two Judges. The Court for Siam, in its turn, ceased to function, except for more or less formal and theoretical purposes, in 1910, when British subjects came under the jurisdiction of special Siamese Courts.

The old British Consular Court was a very fine institution. It did a lot of work, and did it well. Until the year 1903 cases were tried in the Consular office, and this work occupied most of the time of the Consul and of one Consular Assistant, who acted as Registrar. There were several tens of thousands of British subjects under the Court's jurisdiction, mostly Indians, Burmese and Shans, with a fair sprinkling of Singapore and Hongkong Chinese, Malays and Britishers.

The Siamese Government, when they concluded the 1855 Treaty with Great Britain, and similar treaties with the United States, France and other powers, were probably rather glad to be rid of the responsibility of trying foreigners, who were at that time not very numerous, and whose cases, in those more primitive times, might have caused a good deal of friction if tried in the Siamese courts. But the annexation of Annam and Cambodia by France and of Upper Burma by Great Britain resulted in such a big increase in the number of foreign subjects in Siam, all exempt from the jurisdiction of the national courts, that the Siamese Government was very seriously hampered thereby. However, they did the sensible thing. They set to work with a will to reform and reorganise their own tribunals, and as a result they are now, as they deserve to be, masters in their own house.

The British Consular judges all co-operated well with the Siamese authorities, and gave, I think, general satisfaction to British subjects, though few of them had any legal qualifications.

One of my former colleagues—a barrister—once remarked on the bench: "Law and common sense are synonymous terms." He was, of course, quite wrong. Law and common sense are *not* synonymous terms, though Law and Tripe very often are. *Justice* and common sense are synonymous terms, and any man possessing a little common sense can administer good justice, though he may sometimes need to get round the law in order to do so.

Speaking for myself, I was Registrar of the Bangkok Court from 1903 to 1905, and in that capacity tried most of the smaller cases, and I ran a Consular Court of my own at Singora in 1908 and 1909. With all due modesty, I may say that I received great praise for my judicial work, very few of my decisions were appealed against, and not a single one reversed on appeal. I attained this happy result in spite of the fact that I always circumvented the Law when I thought it desirable to do so in the interests of justice.

Of course, a Consular Judge had to *know* some law, otherwise he could not circumvent it, nor could he tackle the barristers and solicitors who practised before him. The first time that I, then a lad of twenty-two, with no special legal training, had to try a case in which two tough old barristers were appearing, I felt some inward trepidation. However, I mugged up the law over-night, and being possessed of a certain amount of cheek, I soon snuffed out both the legal luminaries. From that time onwards, I never bothered my head

Signature above, Chulalongkorn, R.S.
Signature below, Devawongse Varoparkar, Foreign Minister

Translation:

(Manu Regia) Chulalonkorn R.S.

Somdetch Phra Paramindr Maha Chulalonkorn Phra Chula Chom Klao King of Siam, both Northern and Southern and all its Dependencies Laos Chiang, Laos Kow, Malays, Kareans, &c, &c, &c,

To all and singular to whom these presents shall come

Know Ye!

Whereas We having had duly examined the Commission dated first day of July 1905 by which His Majesty Edward VII King of the United Kingdom of Great Britain and Ireland etc. etc. etc. has nominated William Alfred Rae Wood Esquire, Vice-Consul for the United Kingdom (in the district of Chieng mai, including Laken Lam-poonchi, han Thoy, Phre, Lahong, Swlakelop, Sukotai, Pitsanulok and Pichai in) Siam and being willing to treat W. A. R. Wood Esquire — favourably authorizes him to exercise the functions which are entrusted to him in the interest of the British seamen and merchants and to have all the privileges, immunities and precedence of his employment, according to Treaty engagements. All Administrative and Judicial Authorities are commanded to recognise him in the capacity of Vice-Consul for the United Kingdom of Great Britain in order that he may be able freely to exercise the said Consular functions provided always for his personal business relations he may be sued without the right to claim any privileges of exemption.

The said authorities are enjoined to attend to the execution of the present authorization which shall be registered wherever it may be necessary.

Done at the Court of Chakrakri Hall, Grand Palace, Bangkok, this twenty fifth day of December ———————— of the year Ratana Koslndr Sok 124. (1905) being the 13355 8th day of our Reign:

By His Majesty's Command.

Devawongse Varoprakar

about lawyers, even when they got the better of me, as happened now and then.

I did not much like European or American lawyers, because few of them understood Siamese or any other Oriental language, and as only about five per cent of the evidence was given in English, hours had to be wasted in interpretation for their benefit. In cases in which no counsel appeared—and these were the most numerous—I was ready to hear evidence in any language which I and the parties understood, taking it down direct in English.

Consuls with legal minds were sometimes terrified, I found, of hearing anything in their Consular capacity which might possibly prejudice their decisions as Judges, and when some unfortunate British subject came in to seek advice, they would break out into a cold sweat, fearing that they were about to have their minds infected with the germs of prejudice in respect of some possible future legislation. Now jurymen, who are not trained to keep open minds, must, I suppose, be protected against outside information, but as for myself, I always kept my eyes and ears open, in and out of Court, just as every businessman does in regard to business matters, and I do not believe that anyone ever suffered any injustice thereby. Quite the contrary.

"But," my legal friends will exclaim, raising their hands in horror, "judicial cognizance should never be taken of any matter which has not been deposed to on oath, and is therefore EVIDENCE."

Well, all I can say is that I early acquired a contempt for many of the legal conventions concerning evidence on oath, and an even greater contempt for oaths. A man who intends to tell the truth will tell it, whether he be sworn or not, a man who goes to a court to lie will lie though he be sworn in a hundred different ways. This is particularly true of British courts, where the oath is often administered rather hurriedly and informally. In Siamese courts the oath is a somewhat more impressive affair, and a few extra susceptible witnesses may perhaps be frightened thereby into comparative veracity; but not many.

Of course, now and then in a lifetime one meets with a man who really stands in awe of some particular form of oath. I remember an amusing case of this. It was not uncommon for an Indian plaintiff to offer to withdraw his claim if the defendant would deny his liability on oath. This always seemed to me a foolish thing to do, but apparently the thought that the other fellow was consigning himself to hell was more pleasing than the problematical chance of getting back the money. In the case referred to, the defendant, on being challenged to swear, offered to take any kind of oath that he did not owe the plaintiff a single cent. "Would you swear on the waters of the Ganges?" asked the plaintiff. "Certainly I would, if there were any of it here," was the reply, "but as there isn't, I shall have to swear on something else." "That's just where you're mistaken," said the wily plaintiff, "I've been getting ready for this case." Then, producing from his bosom a small bottle of muddy water, he held it up before his astonished opponent. "Now then," said he, "swear on that if you dare." "No," gasped the defendant, "I'll pay up." And pay up he did.

I was told later that the water came from the canal behind the court.

We have all been told that the jury system is one of the bulwarks of an Englishman's liberties. Undoubtedly it often enables him to remain at liberty when he would be much better locked up. Under the Siam Order in Council provision was made for a jury of five in certain cases, and we used to draw five names from a hat whenever an important criminal case was to be tried, or when one of the parties to a big civil case applied for a jury. I fancy that the jurors summoned rarely believed, in their hearts, that their names had been drawn from a hat, but were inclined to flatter themselves that they had been specially singled out owing to their uncanny acumen in dealing with the particular matter at issue. This sometimes led them into pitfalls.

There used to be a gay spark named Mat Ali, of Malay origin, who was the head of a secret society in Bangkok at the end of last century, when secret societies were all the go. He was always being charged with murder, either as principal or accessory, he always engaged the same counsel, he always pleaded an alibi, and the jury always let him off. However, by the time he was charged with his sixth murder, his alibis were getting known to possible jurors, and were becoming a bit fly-blown, especially as he had used one particular alibi twice over. It was a beautiful alibi, specially designed to be cross-examination-proof. Mat Ali was alleged to have been participating, at the time when the crime was committed, in a tug-of-war. In the case of an ordinary alibi, the various witnesses may be cross-examined as to what the accused and the other witnesses were doing, and they often contradict one another. But the tug-of-war alibi is comparatively safe. "What was the prisoner doing?" "Pulling the rope." "What was A. doing?" "Pulling the rope." "How about B., C. and D.?" "All pulling hard." "And you yourself?" "Pulling hardest of all."

The jury empanelled for Mat Ali's sixth murder trial had got wind of the fact that the tug-of-war alibi was to be tried once again, and they were determined to have none of it. When the case for the prosecution was finished, the foreman of the jury at once rose to his feet and said: "Your Honour, we have heard enough of this case, and are prepared to give our verdict now." The Consul, surprised, for the evidence was strong, asked: "Am I to understand that you desire to acquit the prisoner without calling upon him for his defence?" "On the contrary, Your Honour, we unanimously find him GUILTY," replied the foreman, with tremendous emphasis.

"May I ask, Your Honour," quietly remarked the prisoner's lawyer, "to make a note of the fact that the jury desires to find my client guilty without hearing a word of his defence. I am calling twenty-eight most reputable witnesses to prove that my client was taking part in a tug-of-war at the very moment when the crime was committed."

So the jury had to listen to the whole tug-of-war alibi from beginning to end. They then once more found the prisoner guilty. He of course appealed on the ground that the jury had displayed prejudice against him, and was acquitted.

In this case the Consul would have done better to have discharged the jury before hearing the defence, and retried the case with a fresh jury. In another case the jury waited until the end before giving their little performance. This was a charge against a member of a rival secret society for shooting one of Mat Ali's adherents. Most of the tram drivers and conductors belonged to Mat Ali's society, and their rivals took to lurking down side lanes, and potting at them with revolvers. Two drivers were killed and several passengers wounded, and people got so scared that the authorities had to provide armed guards on every tramcar. At last an Indian British subject was arrested on suspicion of having shot one of the drivers, and was brought before a jury in the British Consular Court. At the end of the trial, the jury found him guilty, but spoilt it all by adding the following rider: "In ordinary circumstances, we should have thought the evidence hardly strong enough to justify a conviction, but in view of the prevalence of this sort of crime in Bangkok, we consider it desirable to make an example of somebody."

This prisoner likewise, I need hardly say, brought off a successful appeal.

I remember the foreman of one jury, who was manager of a firm of importers, seizing the opportunity to advertise goods in which he was interested. Mention by a witness of machinery belting called forth an enquiry as to whether it was Bilton's belting, a typist was asked whether he used Tinkleton's typewriters, and a carpenter was tackled concerning Sercomb's circular saws. The foreman drew blank every time, whereupon he groaned and shook his head at his fellow jurors, as much as to say: "What reliance can be felt for witnesses who don't use Bilton's belting, Tinkleton's typewriters, or Sercomb's circular saws?"

A method sometimes used by wily counsel for bamboozling innocent jurymen consisted in calling one respectable witness among a crowd of ruffians to prove an alibi. I was myself used for this purpose on one occasion. I happened to have been present at a big entertainment given by one of the King's brothers on the night when a murder was committed. The murderer, on being brought to trial, pleaded that he had been present at the entertainment in question. Fourteen villains were hired to swear that they had seen him there, and finally I was put into the witness-box for the same purpose. I had *not* seen him there, and said so, but was lured into saying that I could not swear he was *not* there. Counsel then addressed the jury as follows: "I have called fifteen witnesses, of whom fourteen swear that they actually saw my client at the entertainment given by Prince X. Mr. Wood, my fifteenth witness, is no less a person than the Registrar of this Court, and is therefore entitled to your special attention. He did not, it is true, actually notice my client, but he was very definite in denying that he had *not* seen him. His evidence is, therefore, of a nature to add great weight to that of my other witnesses."

The prisoner got off.

We kept a Consular jail in the Legation compound, with two British constables and two native warders in charge. At times there were as many as forty or fifty prisoners in the jail, at other times very few. No allowance was at that time granted us for the upkeep of the grounds of the Legation, but they were always maintained in excellent order by prison labour, and we regarded a lack of convicts as rather a disaster. One Consul is alleged to have replied, when a man brought before him for some petty offence begged to be let off with a fine: "Do not talk such ridiculous nonsense. We have only five prisoners in the jail, and we have to get the compound ready for Queen Victoria's birthday next week."

It was not extraordinarily difficult to escape from the Consular jail, as the prisoners used to do work all over the compound, and usually only had two men looking after them.

We did not worry ourselves overmuch when a prisoner fled, unless he was a really dangerous man, or unless the *Siam Free Press* tried to be funny about the matter. One half-Indian lad named Kadersah escaped from our jail no less than eleven times. Nobody really objected very much to his escaping, if only he would have kept away, even for a few months; but as soon as he got out, he invariably stole something and was promptly arrested and brought back. We tried deporting him to Singapore, but he returned on the next steamer. He was a very nice boy, and I once appealed to him, as a personal favour, either to remain out of jail, or else stay there when he was put in. He promised me to do his best, but said that he feared it might be difficult to oblige me, as there were so many things to steal, and so many ways out of jail, and he could not resist the excitement of stealing or the fun of running away from jail. In the end, he died of cholera. When dying, he sent me a message to thank me for having been so kind to him, and to apologise for having been such a nuisance, adding: "But I couldn't help it; I was born that way."

We had to carry out our own executions. I am thankful to say that I myself never had occasion to hang a man, but it fell to the lot of two of my colleagues to do so. On one occasion four men, all Pathans, were hanged on the same day. They had murdered five of their compatriots—one of those vendetta affairs common in North-West India. Great preparations had to be made, building a special gallows, weighing the prisoners and then testing the ropes with sacks of sand of the same weight as each of them. It was a very harrowing affair. Three of the prisoners died bravely, admitting the justice of their sentence, and standing to attention when the fatal moment came. The fourth protested his innocence, screamed and cried for mercy, and had to be dragged to the scaffold.

It is not a very pleasant job, hanging a man, but it was all part of the day's work for a British Consul in Siam when I was young.

We had some curious jailers. On one occasion the first and

second jailers were with difficulty prevented from fighting a duel with revolvers, the first jailer having cast aspersions on the character of his colleague's wife. The second jailer later explained to me that he thought it extremely vulgar of the first jailer to say nasty things about his wife, though, he added, it was all true. "She's been unfaithful to me, Sir, reg'lar and systematic for fifteen years past, and I was getting used to it. But I *did* think it 'ard that she should ask my son, a lad of twelve, to pull the punkah while she was carrying on with a Me'omedan."

One of this worthy's successors had greater faith in his spouse. He went to India on six months' furlough, and six months after his return his wife presented him with an heir. Far from feeling in any degree suspicious, he was never tired of boasting that he was the father of a twelve months' child. "That sort are very rare, Your Honour, but there have been several of them in our family, and all fine, strong babies."

The lady who had the *affaire* with the Me'omedan ended up by running away, and went to assist in the management of a "bar" kept by an elderly lady who was a great thorn in my side. This old dame could never get anyone to pay for drinks consumed unless she sued them, so had to spend about half her time in the Consular Court. The poor old thing always wept throughout the proceedings. On one occasion she lost her case. This caused her to faint away, and I had to take her over to my house and revive her with brandy. Another time an irritable customer cracked her over the head with a bottle, and she appeared in my dining-room during dinner, covered with blood and screeching horribly. She declined to be washed or bandaged until I had brought the Consul to have a look at the blood.

This was less embarrassing than the request made to me by a much younger lady, inhabiting a rival "bar". She had taken part in a scrap, and had been forcibly seated on a chair on which there happened to be a broken glass. Her garb being somewhat diaphanous, she got quite badly cut, and appeared next day in my office, loudly demanding that I should examine her injuries then and there.

This "showing of blood" was very common among Indians. After a fight they would smear blood all over their faces and bodies, and plaster it in their hair and beards. If necessary, they would keep it over from Saturday till Monday—or Tuesday, if a Bank Holiday intervened—so as to harrow the Consul's feelings and induce him to give a thumping big sentence to the other fellow.

My elderly lady friend was not really much hurt by the bottle, but on another occasion a Maltese British subject burst into my dining-room during dinner, lay down on the floor, and expired. He had been stabbed in a brawl in one of the local bars. The poor fellow tried to tell me who had stabbed him, but could not articulate properly, and we never succeeded in discovering who was responsible for his death.

Consular Officers were sent now and then to hold District Courts in outlying parts of Siam where there were large numbers of British subjects. The ruby and sapphire mining district of Pailin and Nawong, south-east of Bangkok, contained several thousand British subjects, nearly all Shans, and I was sent there to hold a court three years running, in 1903, 1904 and 1905. It was a most interesting experience for a young fellow. The Shans were in many ways as tough a crowd as could have been found in any of Bret Harte's mining camps, but at the same time very unsophisticated and full of fun and jollity. The mining villages, set among little green hills, were perfect gems of scenic beauty. I soon found that I could make the miners do almost anything I wanted, mainly by laughing and joking with them, and taking part in their little ceremonies and jollifications.

The amount of work one managed to get through at Pailin was astounding. It was quite usual to register several hundred newcomers in a day, and as each registration certificate bore a full description of the holder in English and Siamese, and each applicant had to be sworn, this took up some time. In addition, all the year's litigation had been bottled up ready for the Consular Officer—murder, right of way, irrigation disputes, libel, abduction, and especially complaints of encroachments on other people's mining rights.

On one occasion I had made arrangements to leave for the coast the next morning, and had sat up till eleven at night, trying what I thought was my last case for that year. At 1 a.m. I was called up by a Shan who had been cracked on the head by a compatriot with a piece of firewood. The cause of the trouble was that the prosecutor had taken me out shooting, which was looked upon by the aggressor as a sign of arrogance which ought not to be tolerated. I sent for the offender, opened the Court again at 2.30 a.m., heard six witnesses, and at 3.30 sentenced my man to five days' hard labour. The hard labour consisted in helping to carry my luggage to the coast, and as we only took four days, I remitted one day of the sentence for good conduct. The prisoner took a great liking to me, and insisted on accompanying me to Bangkok, where he remained as my servant for several years.

In the year 1902, as mentioned above, the Consular Court at Bangkok went up a step, and became His Britannic Majesty's Court for Siam, with a real barrister as Judge. We built a fine new court-house, and had a lovely lion and unicorn put over the bench, but I really do not think that much public advantage was gained by the change.

One of our new judges fell foul of a section of the local Press, and we made quite a lot of money by fining newspapermen for contempt of court. The climax was reached by the publication of a leading article wherein unfavourable comparisons were drawn between Judge H. and Judge Jeffreys. The offending editor was hauled up before me in custody, protesting that he would not withdraw a single word, but after a long private conference, in which Mrs. Editor took part, I persuaded him to think better of it.

I may remark that Judge H. did not really bear the slightest resemblance to Judge Jeffreys, being the kindest-hearted and

Theatrical dancers

The astrologer, telling fortunes,
selling charms and amulets.
A common street scene.

A wedding couple, hands raised for guests to pour lustral water.

ABOVE: The ghosts start on their journey down river. Sorcerer standing, reading scroll. Three young musicians to the left.

LEFT: Spirit raft on journey to Bangkok. It contained a good supply of food as spirit must not be straved.

most generous man in the world, though a bit impulsive at times. I lived with him, and ran all the household affairs, and I used to get very much upset by his indiscriminate hospitality. He would ask me to have dinner ready for six bachelors, having in fact invited a far larger number of people, and forgotten all about it. When the time came, thirty or more guests would appear, including perhaps several married couples and a Royal Highness or two. I always kept a big supply of canned provisions in the house.

I was Registrar of the new British Court for two years, and acted twice as Judge. As Registrar, I tried most of the petty cases, heard judgment summonses, taxed bills of costs, and conducted the preliminary enquiry in serious criminal cases. I was also Official Receiver in Bankruptcy. On Fridays I used to try small civil claims, and on Saturdays petty criminal charges, averaging about twelve to fifteen cases a day. Besides this, I was in charge of most of the estates of deceased British subjects, and had a large number of children to look after, educate, and give in marriage. I wish I could be as successful with my own investments as I was with theirs.

Nothing gives me greater happiness than to reflect on the good fortune which placed me in a position where for over thirty years I was able to be of some use to a number of young people of all races, and to save them from being fleeced and plundered—often, alas! by their own relations. Consular jurisdiction in regard to Probate and Administration long outlived the Consular Court's jurisdiction in other matters. I say with pride that Consular Officers in Siam performed this duty well.

My greatest joy was to arrange marriages between my young heirs and heiresses, pool their money, invest it for them, and launch them on the sea of life together. All the marriages arranged by me turned out well.

If any of my babies—now, many of them, grandparents— should happen to read these lines, I beg them to believe that I loved them all well, and the naughty boys best of all.

When I was stationed at Singora as Vice-Consul from 1908 to 1911, I was in charge of the only Consular Court which had up to that time been seen in that district. My Court was looked upon by British subjects as a nice new toy, and they patronised it extensively. Besides a Court, I also ran a football club, and we played soccer twice a week in the local bull-ring. Keenness on football was understood to be a means of gaining my affection, and when a new player appeared, I always assumed that he was a party to a prospective case in the Consular Court. I believe that it was generally supposed that no litigant could possibly win a case unless he had kicked at least three goals. For this reason, litigants were always rather rough players.

At Singora I had a most intelligent Malay servant named Che Leh. He was a retired actor, and could do almost anything on earth. Once I had occasion to sentence a stalwart Pathan to six months hard labour, and as I had no suitable jail accommodation for a comparatively long term prisoner, I decided to send him to Bangkok, a journey of four days by sea. I therefore put Che Leh into a khaki uniform, pinned a badge on to his cap, handed him a rifle and a sheet of blue paper, and said to him: "Che Leh, I appoint you Chief Constable of His Majesty's Court. Take this prisoner to Bangkok and hand him over to the British Consul-General there. Here is your warrant."

Che Leh saluted and set off without delay, though he could not speak a word of Siamese, and he carried out the job without any hitch. When, on his return, I praised him for his smart work, he replied: "Why, Sir, that's nothing at all. Shall it be said that I, famed throughout the Peninsula for my rendering of the part of the ghost of Hamlet's father, cannot take on the part of a mere policeman ?"

This reminds me that I was once privileged to see Che Leh in the part of Hamlet's father's ghost. He acted by special request at a benefit performance given for a Malay tragedienne who wore tinted glasses and had no front teeth. Che Leh was robed in a white nighty, clanked a chain, and had a bloody dagger sticking in his bosom. I asked him later about the dagger, which puzzled me, as we had seen Hamlet's father dying in the prologue from the effects of about four gallons of poison, poured into his ear through a gigantic funnel. Che Leh explained, however, that every ghost always had to have a bloody dagger sticking in its bosom, otherwise the audience might not know that it *was* a ghost.

I used to settle far more cases than I ever decided. I found that in money claims a settlement could often be made by getting the defendant to make what I thought a fair offer, and if this were refused I would postpone the case till the next day, have the money brought along and jingle it in a bag under the nose of the plaintiff. He almost always took it. If notes were brought, I always insisted on small denominations, and spread them all over my desk for the plaintiff to look at. It is wonderful how tempting a large number of small notes look when artistically spread out.

Another good way of settling cases is by laughing with the parties—never at them. Siam is the land of laughter, and a smile or a chuckle at the right moment often has power to remove what seemed insuperable obstacles. This does not apply to cases between ladies. They never seem able to see how funny it is when people will not pay them what is owing to them.

If one of a couple of British subjects whose dispute I had almost settled ever said to me: "All right, Sir, I agree; but first let me consult my father (or brother, uncle or nephew, as the case might be) I would at once acquiesce. But if it was a mother, grandmother, aunt, niece or sister, or, worst of all, a mother-in-law who had to be consulted, then I would give up my attempt at conciliation, and went on with the case to the bitter end.

Of mothers-in-law, more elsewhere.

III

Safe Custody

In the last chapter I mentioned the ruby and sapphire mines at Pailin and Nawong, and the District Courts which British Consular Officers used formerly to hold there.

Until about the end of the last century, the big community of Burmese and Shan British subjects living at Pailin was ruled, almost in a despotic manner, by an old Burman named Maung Kaing, who had been appointed British Headman by some almost pre-historic British Consul. Maung Kaing, though he had really no legal jurisdiction, tried all cases himself, according to a code of laws of his own invention. When he died, just before my arrival in Siam, the British Consul decided to place the administration of justice at Pailin on a more regular footing, so a Vice-Consul was sent to hold a proper court there, and to appoint a new Headman with very limited powers.

This new Headman, a Shan named Puchong Saw, seems to have been appointed because he had more money than anyone else at the mines. He soon showed signs of an intention to ignore all rules and regulations, and to rule the miners even more despotically than Maung Kaing had done. Now Maung Kaing, though a tyrant, had been a just tyrant, and was respected by all the people at Pailin. Nobody ever dreamed of complaining against him; but Puchong Saw was a very different sort of man, and petitions against him were constantly being sent to the British Consul at Bangkok.

The first time I visited Pailin, in the year 1903, I received orders to keep a very sharp eye on Puchong Saw, and I was authorised, if necessary, to dismiss him from the post of Headman, and to appoint another man in his place.

On meeting Puchong Saw I noticed that he wore his silk turban very low down over his left ear, completely concealing it, and I soon heard from some of his enemies—who were numerous—that he had formerly been the chief of a gang of dacoits in the Shan States during the reign of King Theebaw of Burma. He had been captured by one of the Shan princes, and had been nailed by his left ear to a post. However, he had broken loose during the night, leaving his ear nailed to the post. Hence his original manner of fixing his turban.

I had only been a few days at Pailin when an old Shan miner named Kham Oo was cruelly beaten up and wounded by two young ruffians named Sang Lai and Sang Suk, who were hangers-on of the Headman. It appeared that old Kham Oo had a difference of opinion with the Headman about the water channel which he used to irrigate his small mine, and had ventured to say that he intended to complain to me. Thereupon Puchong Saw sent his two henchmen to give Kham Oo a lesson. The lesson consisted in stabbing him in five places and breaking two of his ribs.

I at once instructed Puchong Saw to arrest the two culprits. He refused, saying that they were men of the highest character and were innocent of the offence charged against them. I therefore issued a warrant for their arrest, and went along to see it executed. We found Sang Lai without difficulty, but Sang Suk could not be found, and I was told he was hiding in the Headman's house. When I went to ask him about this, he admitted that Sang Suk had spent the night in his house, but said that he had just left. Thereupon I summarily dismissed Puchong Saw from his post of Headman of Pailin, and appointed an elderly Burmese mine-owner in his stead.

A few days later I had to leave Pailin for Nawong, four days march away. I had already committed Sang Lai for trial before a jury in Bangkok, on a charge of attempted murder,

so had to take him with me. I took every precaution to see
that he did not escape, having been warned that a rescue
might be attempted. He was made to wear handcuffs all
the time, and I had two armed men watching him day and
night.

There was a mining village called Hua Kiong, situated
about half-way between Pailin and Nawong, also presided
over by a Shan Headman. When I approached Hua Kiong,
the Headman and many of the miners, as was usual, came
out to meet me. I asked the Headman whether there were any
cases to be tried. He replied that there had been no crime
during the past year until the night before, when one man
had stabbed another.

"I hope you have got the offender locked up in safe custody,"
said I.

"Oh, yes, Sir," he replied, "he is not exactly locked up, but
he is in safe custody, all right. I have got him nailed by his ear
to one of the posts of my house."

"Great Heavens!" I exclaimed, "Do you call that safe
custody? Have you never heard of Puchong Saw, who left the
Shan States to become Headman at Pailin, leaving his ear
behind him?"

"Do not be anxious," said the Headman, "I have placed my
son in charge of the prisoner. He is twelve years old, and is a
very trustworthy boy."

As he spoke these words, a small figure hove into sight some
way along the road—the trustworthy boy in person. He came
tearing along at a frantic speed, his turban in his hand and his
long hair streaming behind him, and when he came near
enough to be heard be cried out:

"He has gone, he has gone! He broke loose, leaving his ear
on the post; then he knocked me down, and escaped!"

Words failed me. I gave a sign to proceed to the village, and
on we went. When we reached the Headman's house, there I
saw the ear. It clung, in all its gory horror, to one of the house
posts.

At first I was filled with rage. Then I saw how extraordinarily amusing it was, so I sat down and laughed until I cried; and all the Shans, to whom laughter and tears come equally readily, stood around and laughed with me. The trustworthy boy laughed loudest of all.

"Mr. Headman," I said as soon as I had regained my powers of speech, "you made a big mistake. Your ideas about safe custody are out of date, and consequently your prisoner has escaped. But anyhow part of him is here, and it is my duty to arrest as much of him as I can find. Take that ear down, salt it, and I shall transport it to Bangkok."

He did as I instructed him; but when I gave it to the British Consul at Bangkok, he did not laugh nearly so heartily as I had done.

I only stayed one day at Hua Klong, and then went on to Nawong. At Nawong there was yet another Shan Headman. As soon as I met him, I said: "I have with me a prisoner who has to stand his trial on a grave charge. What arrangements can you make for keeping him in safe custody while I am here?"

He replied, "I have no very secure place in which to confine a prisoner. I have, however, some very large, strong nails. I suggest nailing him by his ear to a post."

The Headman seemed quite taken aback when I sat down and roared with laughter. "No, no," I exclaimed; "I ought to be taking three prisoners to Bangkok, but have only one, so can take no risks. I have no faith at all in the ear-nailing system of safe custody. Puchong Saw was nailed by his ear to a post in the Shan States; he left his ear there and escaped to Pailin, where he became Headman, and has caused me endless trouble. An offender at Hua Kiong, secured by the same method, and guarded by a very trustworthy boy, escaped only three days ago. I have his ear, salted, in my pocket at this moment. No more nails and posts for me!"

So we had to secure our solitary prisoner by more prosaic and modern methods. These proved so successful that he was

at length brought safely to the coast at Chantaboon and taken
on board the little steamer which ran once weekly to Bangkok.
The steamer was not due to leave until the next day, so I
arranged that I and my party, including the prisoner Sang Lai,
should sleep on board. As I had ascertained that Sang Lai could
not swim, I thought this a pretty safe plan, and was even so
confident that I took off his handcuffs. And what was the
result? As soon as it was dusk, he leapt overboard, though he
could not swim a stroke, and the sea was infested with sharks.

How we got him out of the water I cannot remember; but
we did it somehow. Then I, being the only person on board
who knew anything about artificial respiration, had to spend
half the night in resuscitating him.

"What a fool!" thought I, as I worked Sang Lai's arms up
and down, "I am taking him to spend about three years in a
nice, airy jail, without too much work to do, and with plenty
of food to eat, yet he prefers to risk drowning or being eaten
by a shark. What a fool!"

That is what I thought then. I am not quite so sure now. I
have spent three years and three months in the lock-up.

IV

Siamese Courts and Justice

My principal experience of Siamese Courts of Law has been in connection with the so-called International Courts, which tried cases in which British subjects were concerned.

The first International Court in Siam was at Chiengmai. It was instituted as a result of the Anglo-Siamese Treaty of 1883, and the system was later extended to the whole of Siam. A British Consular Officer was entitled to sit in any case, civil or criminal, in which a British subject was concerned, whether as plaintiff or defendant, to ask such questions and make such suggestions as he might think necessary in the interests of justice, to file a written opinion for the use of the Appeal Court, and, finally, to withdraw to the Consular Court and try by himself any case in which a British subject was the defendant or accused.

Appeals were heard by the British Consul-General at Bangkok in collaboration with a delegate of the Siamese Ministry of Justice.

This system, with modifications, was extended to the whole of Siam by the Anglo-Siamese Treaty of 1909. Under that Treaty, appeals were heard by the Siamese Court of Appeal, with the collaboration of a European legal adviser.

European legal advisers had, I may say, been engaged by Siam long before 1909, and were employed in several of the Bangkok courts, as well as in the International Courts in the north. In the northern International Courts the first advisers made their appearance in 1905, twenty-two years after the courts were inaugurated.

The law administered by the International Courts was Siamese law, with a proviso that English law was to be followed in cases where there was no Siamese law which could be applied. In the early days it was often found necessary to apply English law in matters of contract, partnership, domicile, etc., and English rules of evidence were followed to a great extent.

The International Court system came to an end in 1925. The Treaty signed in that year did, it is true, grant to British Consular Officers some powers of interference in Siamese courts, but in practice these powers have never been exercised, and were of no real importance.

I sat in the International Courts at Chiengmai and Nan in 1905, 1906 and 1907, at Singora in 1910 and 1911, and again at Chiengmai and Lampang from 1912 to 1925, so that I can fairly claim that my personal experience of Siamese courts and justice greatly exceeds that of any other Consular Officer either before or since my time.

The International Court system, all things considered, worked extraordinarily well, and there was seldom any serious friction between Siamese Judges and British Consular Officers. The right to evoke a case from the Siamese International Court and try it in the British Consular Court, the exercise of which would naturally have been somewhat wounding to Siamese *amour propre,* was very rarely exerciscd, and then only in regard to Probate and Administration cases in which it was difficult to apply ordinary Siamese law, or in which dissatisfied claimants were, in effect, trying to use the International Court as a Court of Appeal against the division of an estate already made by a Consular Officer.

In the early days, some Siamese Judges were, perhaps, rather apt to look upon the British Consul as an advocate, whose business it was to get the best possible terms for British litigants; I myself found now and then that a suggestion on my part that a British offender deserved a harsher punishment than that which the Court proposed to inflict caused some surprise. But I hope, and believe, that the Siamese authorities soon saw that all we desired to do was to secure a fair deal for all, irrespective of race; and still more, to help to improve and develop the administration of justice in the Siamese courts, always looking forward to the day when the British Government would feel justified in relinquishing all our powers of interference.

Much praise has been given, and rightly so, to the foreign legal advisers, engaged and paid by Siam, for their share in developing and perfecting the Siamese tribunals; but very little thanks has ever been given to British Consular Officers for performing, for a much longer period, equally useful functions, at no cost to Siam, and in addition to their ordinary Consular duties. Modesty shall not prevent me from saying that I am extremely proud of the part taken by some of my colleagues and myself in this valuable work.

When, after a good deal of experience of Consular Courts, I first made my appearance on the bench of an International Court, I will admit that I found their far more deliberate procedure a little trying. But I soon got used to it, and found, firstly, that parties to cases seem able to put up with a good deal of delay without worrying much, and secondly, that the final decision, even if a bit tardy, was usually just.

There is, perhaps, rather less formality about a Siamese court than a British court. For instance, it is quite usual for Judges to smoke while trying cases, and advocates and litigants are also permitted to do so, or to chew betel-nut if so disposed. When I was young, betel-nut chewing was almost universal, and I was sometimes fain to demand that witnesses should be made to get rid of their quids for my benefit, not because I was so foolish as to see disrespect where none was intended, but because I could not understand what they were saying. I admit with a blush of shame that I still, after sixty-eight years in Siam, am unable to understand the language when spoken with a betel-nut accent. However, it does not matter much now, for few people except aged gaffers and crones chew in these more enlightened days.

I have sat on the bench with more than forty Siamese judges, and looking back, I can say that the great majority of them were very intelligent and cultivated men, conscientious in their work, and pleasant in their manners. One or two of them were, perhaps, a little overbearing at times, and a few may have been a trifle archaic in their outlook, but the proportion of good against—let us say—indifferent judges was certainly enormous.

Of foreign legal advisers I have met all kinds. Those who knew law but no Siamese, those who knew Siamese but no law, those who knew both, and those who knew neither. Those who quarrelled with the judges, those who quarrelled with me, those who quarrelled with everybody, and those who quarrelled with nobody. But after making due allowance for the idiosyncrasies and foibles of some foreign advisers, the fact remains that, as a body, they did very good work for Siam, and were of great assistance in tiding over a difficult period.

There are no juries in Siam, and I will admit that it has never occurred to me, in any one of the hundreds of cases in which I have taken part in Siamese courts, that any advantage would have been gained had a jury been available. In fact, I do not think much of juries.

It is a curious fact that certain races seem to be naturally inclined towards litigation. Nothing need surprise one in an individual—Dr. Johnson collected orange peel and the Roman Emperor Domitian spent most of his spare time catching flies—but weird tastes which extend to whole communities seem difficult to explain. Now a lawsuit, in any country, takes up a good deal of time, costs a lot of money, is very worrying, and quite often fails to bring about the result aimed at. Why, therefore, should whole races prefer this form of amusement to any other? Quite impossible to say.

Certain of the races of India are extraordinarily addicted to litigation, and some of their members can be seen almost any day hanging about most Siamese Courts. In Siam, besides ordinary disputes, some Indians get involved in peculiar matrimonial troubles. Many of them are too ready to be jealous of their Siamese or Lao wives. In India and Pakistan the liberty of women is still to some extent restricted, while in Siam women are quite free. The mild flirtations of perfectly respectable women are apt to shock many Indians, but the flightiness of the rather naughty ladies they sometimes wed rouses them to fury, and all sorts of complications are the result. In the next chapter I will give a few examples of this.

A case in which an Indian husband really had some cause for jealousy was one in which a man, returning home unexpectedly, found a young man in his wife's mosquito net with her. He charged them with adultery, which they both denied, alleging that they were harmlessly engaged in catching mosquitoes. The judge enquired whether they had caught many, but they rather wistfully replied that they had only had time to catch one. They were just going to catch another when the husband came in and interrupted them.

Another curious Indian case was one in which an elderly and most respectable Mahomedan was charged with breaking a compatriot's arm with a heavy bludgeon. His defence was to the following effect: "The thing was a complete accident. I had absolutely no intention of injuring the man's arm in any way. My intention was to crack his skull open, but he foolishly interposed his arm, which accidentally received the blow."

I remember also a young Burmese who, when charged with stealing a bottle of whisky from a store, pleaded that he had taken it by accident, mistaking it for something of his own. "What did you mistake it for?" asked the Judge; "Your cigarette case?" "Oh, no, Sir," he replied; "Of course nobody could mistake a bottle of whisky for a cigarette case. I mistook it for my pocket handkerchief."

Another Burmese was once charged with illicit gambling. The police raided his house and found a large number of people there, cards and all complete, but the owner of the house had disappeared. Eventually he was found seated astride on top of the roof. When charged, he denied that he knew anything about the gambling. "Then why did you escape on to the roof?" he was asked. "Escape," said he, "I didn't escape. I just went up to sit there. And why shouldn't I? It's my own roof, isn't it?"

Until recently, country people in Siam sometimes wanted to enter charges in Siamese Courts of causing death or sickness by means of witchcraft. The Siamese *Law on Miscellaneous Matters (Laksana Bet Set)* which dates from A.D. 1359, contains sections dealing with offences of this kind, but for many years past it has not been the practice of Siamese Courts to receive such charges. Quite a number of British subjects have complained to me because they could not obtain legal redress against witches. It is impossible not to feel sympathy with such cases, for the grievance is felt to be real, and primitive people cannot be made to see that prosecutions for witchcraft are unreasonable.

A somewhat similar kind of action is that for causing death by certain smells, popularly supposed to be dangerous to sick persons. A Shan British subject actually entered a case against his Chinese neighbour for causing the death of his wife by burning sesame seeds; these, when burnt, give forth a rather pungent odour. The plaintiff's wife was in childbirth, and his contention was that the defendant burnt the seeds well knowing the woman's condition, and knowing also that the smell was likely to kill her. It would, of course, be quite impossible to produce proper medical evidence to prove that the smell of sesame seed really is fatal in maternity cases.

Another Shan sued a neighbour for causing the death of his little son, who was suffering from fever, by frying sausages next door.

These poor people were very grieved and disappointed because I was unable to support their claims as they expected me to do. The tragedy of it is that very likely the deaths, in both cases, were actually accelerated, if not caused, by the smells complained of. People in Siam are far too fond of discussing a sick person's condition in his presence, not sparing him the gloomiest prognostications, and if a patient be told that a certain odour is likely to prove fatal, very likely it will do so.

I may say that a fear of evil results from quite harmless smells is very common in Siam. A visitor with a drop of perfume on his handkerchief is often, to say the least, extremely unwelcome in a sick-room.

The cases referred to show the sort of difficulties sometimes met with by judges in a country which has had to face, in about sixty years, changes which we English managed to spread over several hundred.

As for witchcraft, there may be something in it, but not, I think, what is popularly supposed. Modern opinion generally recognises the power of mind or suggestion to bring about beneficial results. It is not unreasonable to suppose that these forces may also be misused for injurious purposes.

In Siamese courts the judges conduct the proceedings to a far greater extent than is usual in British courts. The advocates available, except in Bangkok, are not, as a general rule, very highly qualified, and if the examination and cross-examination of witnesses be left to them, one seldom gets anywhere at all.

The first time I sat in an International Court, the judge, after hearing all the evidence, said he would adjourn the case for judgment. "But," whispered I, accustomed to British procedure, "both sides have advocates. Are you not going to let them address the Court?" The judge was rather taken aback, but when I pointed out to him that under the Court Rules counsel had a right to address the Court, he informed both the lawyers that he would hear them the following day. This perturbed them a good bit, as they had never before been called upon to do such a thing. When the appointed time came, one of the lawyers really made a very excellent speech, marshalling the facts in favour of his client with great clearness and conciseness; but the other advocate, with tears in his eyes, explained that he had never made a speech in his life, and was too old to begin. However, he added, producing a document, he had written down all he had to say, and begged the Court to read it over carefully.

After that, I never worried any more about Counsel's speeches.

Until 1934 executions of murderers in Siam were carried out by beheading the prisoner with a sword. Capital punishment was, and is, very rarely inflicted. The courts are allowed to, and often do, inflict various terms of imprisonment for murder, and even when a man is sentenced to death, it is quite likely that one of the Courts of Appeal will reduce the sentence. Two appeals may be made, one to the Appeal Court, and one to the *Dika,* or Supreme Court. The latter court is, in theory, a committee appointed by, and acting directly for, the King, who is himself the supreme arbiter. It will thus easily be understood that the extreme penalty of the law is only inflicted in the case of particularly atrocious murderers.

I myself have only ever witnessed one execution by beheading. It was well carried out, but nevertheless I certainly do not ever wish to witness another. The prisoner was a very pleasant young fellow, whom I knew slightly. He was a Buddhist priest, and had shot another priest dead with a revolver. The dead man had given him some pro-vocation, but in Siam the idea of a priest taking any life, even that of an animal, is abhorrent to every religious sentiment of the people, and for him to slay a human being and a fellow priest is an act which strikes at the very roots of all Buddhist morality.

Before the proceedings began, a chapter of Buddhist priests recited prayers for the prisoner. The latter was then blindfolded, and had pellets of mud put in his ears. I was told that he had been given a drug, and be certainly appeared quite calm and passive. He was permitted to say farewell to his mother—a truly poignant sight—and was then made to sit down, and lightly bound with strips of white cloth to a low wooden framework, which acted as a support for his back. The executioners, two in number, who had till then remained hidden behind a bush, now advanced with a curious dancing motion, waving their swords. They retreated again two or three times, thus producing in the minds of the onlookers a feeling of tension, which in my case was almost unbearable. Finally, one of the executioners rushed at the prisoner and dealt him a tremendous blow with the sword, cutting through the spinal column. The head was not entirely severed, but was cut off quite easily by the other executioner.

The severed head, after being held up on high by the second executioner, was placed on a stake. The body, still shackled, was thrown into a grave, ready dug beforehand. After a few minutes the head was taken from the stake and was also thrown into the grave, which was then filled in.

I remember being very much impressed, when the head was placed on the stake, by the calm and peaceful look on the poor fellow's face. I have seen many dead persons, but not one of their faces bore such a look of calm and innocent sleep as that of the murderer whose head had just been violently struck from his body.

The difficulty about executions with a sword is that too much depends upon human skill and dexterity, which are at best fallible. Moreover, it is repugnant to the nature of most Siamese to take human life in cold blood; it is, therefore, always necessary to give the executioners some sort of stimulant. If too much be given, the result may easily be very terrible.

It will be seen that decapitation is a form of capital punishment which I do not much like. I may as well say that I do not like our English method much better. The French possess, in the guillotine, an instrument with the advantage of mechanical precision, but like all forms of decapitation, it produces too much blood. Many Americans disapprove of the electric chair.

In the year 1934 the Siamese Parliament abolished the system of execution by beheading, and substituted shooting as the law's extreme penalty. Shooting is certainly much better than beheading. It affords less scope for bungling, and does not produce so much blood. Nevertheless, it is not a perfect method, and I have heard of one case at least in which death was not by any means instantaneous.

When I first came to Siam, Siamese jails were not very pleasant places. Most of them were overcrowded and insanitary; and they often contained people who were not really criminals at all; for instance, many people so disliked Courts of Law that they would often run away rather than appear even as witnesses; for this reason, witnesses were frequently arrested, and if the case in which they were required hung fire for a few months, or even years, the unfortunate witnesses might remain locked up indefinitely.

I came across a case of this kind shortly after my arrival in the country. I was travelling by boat on the Mekhlong River near the town of Rajburi, accompanied by an Englishman in the service of the Siamese Government. As we passed near a sandbank in the river, one of a party of prisoners who were working there, all wearing chains, came to the water's edge, knelt down, and raising his hands begged us in piteous tones to stop and hear what he had to say. We stopped the boat to listen to him.

"Sirs," he said, "I implore you to help me if you can. Ten years ago I was arrested as a witness in a charge of cattle theft. The accused man died before the case came up for trial, but I have been kept in prison ever since. This is because I have no powerful or influential friends to apply for my release, and nobody will listen to the complaints of a poor man like me. Unless you can do something for me, I shall remain in prison until I die."

When we returned to Bangkok, my friend brought this matter to the notice of the Minister of Justice, and the poor man was released shortly afterwards. But if we had not chanced to pass by in our boat he might, as he feared, have spent the rest of his life in jail.

All that sort of thing is now merely a memory of the distant past. Nobody goes to jail now unless convicted or formally charged with a real offence, and the jails are, for the most part, well conducted and comparatively comfortable institutions. The convicts are properly fed, and are well looked after both in health and sickness. Medical Officers regularly inspect all the jails, and each jail has some sort of hospital or sanatorium attached.

In former times, all Siamese convicts were compelled to wear shackles on their feet, but these, save in exceptional cases, were quite light, and did not cause serious hardship. The use of shackles was abolished some years ago, and those who predicted that, if this were done, the prisoners would spend all their time escaping, have been confounded, for escapes from jail are no more frequent than of old.

On the whole, Siamese convicts enjoy greater freedom, and lead more natural and human lives than their fellows in England or in British possessions. They are allowed to smoke, and when working are not forbidden to speak to one another. Those employed outside the jail are not punished if they speak to passers-by. When working in the jail, a prisoner is not required to wear special clothes. On a recent visit to the jail at Chiengmai on a very cold morning, I noticed that most of the convicts were wearing comfortable woollen pullovers or jerseys.

When I once visited a British jail I had an uneasy feeling that the inmates, though well treated, were in a sense set apart, and were in some way different from myself. In a Siamese jail, I do not have any such feeling. The convicts are just ordinary men like me, and I can talk to them without any sense of constraint. This is, I think, a very good thing, as Siamese ex-convicts do not tend to lose their humanity or to feel any prison taint.

John Galsworthy wrote a terrible story, in which he depicted the awful effect of prison on the mind of a man who was determined to maintain his self-respect. The most tragic thing about this story is that it might easily be true. But it could, thank God, never be true in Siam.

I know a great deal about Siamese jails, for when I was a Consular Officer I always made a point of inspecting the jail in any place I visited, and speaking to any British subjects who were confined therein. In Chiengmai and Lampang, I always visited the jails about once a month. This I did quite informally, just going along and tapping at the door, and asking: "May I come in ?" No difficulty was ever placed in my way, and I was allowed to wander all over the place. I very rarely saw anything to which reasonable exception could be taken. I often stood and watched the convicts eating their food, which was clean and plentiful. I may add that all British prisoners used to put on weight when in jail.

British Indian prisoners sometimes raised the question of "unclean" food. Caste difficulties once or twice arose in regard to Hindu convicts, but it was Mahomedan prisoners, with their horror of pork, who caused the greatest difficulty. When this point was raised, as frequently happened, the jail authorities always granted leave for the prisoner or prisoners concerned, to prepare their own food, but even then a suspicion often arose that the vessels provided had been contaminated by the hateful pig. I once pointed out to a Mahomedan convict that, as he had pleaded guilty to a charge of burglary, it was unreasonable for him to invoke the authority of the Koran on the food question. The Koran, I remarked, was a good deal more emphatic in its prohibition of theft than in its regulations as to food, and it was inconsistent for a man who had disregarded the former texts to be too particular about the latter. The fact is that I was myself unreasonable in expecting, or professing to expect, any sort of consistency in regard to religious matters. We Christians are just as inconsistent. Christ condemned those who strained at gnats and swallowed camels, but His followers have gone on doing it ever since.

In some Siamese jails, the convicts used to be made to learn off certain particulars concerning themselves, which they were then ready to repeat to any distinguished visitor who might display an interest in them. For instance: "I, Ai Deng, No. 938, age twenty-six, was sentenced on November 7th, 1930 to three years imprisonment for stealing a buffalo. I am due to be released on November 7th, 1934." One Shan convict, in the jail at Phrae for theft, always insisted on adding: "But I didn't do it, all the same." A Prince was about to visit the jail, and I was asked to remonstrate with this prisoner, and to persuade him to give his little recitation nicely, like his comrades. I mentioned the matter to him, and he promised to do his best. However, when the Prince came, he again said: "But I didn't do it, all the same." I heard later that the Prince was so struck by this prisoner's originality that he managed to get part of his sentence remitted. I may as well remark that the man *did* do it, all the same.

When I was visiting a certain Siamese provincial jail, the official who accompanied me showed me a Siamese convict, under sentence of death for murder. I stopped and spoke a few words to the man, who told me that he had lodged an appeal with the Supreme Court, and added that he did not think he ought to be executed, because he had not been actuated by malice towards the man he had killed. "What made you do it, then? " I asked. "Well," he explained, "I was very hard up, and a man who disliked him hired me to do it." I enquired how much he had been paid, and he said he had only received two ticals—about 4s. It was a very poor district, and that year had been a hard one for the peasantry. The convict seemed honestly to think that he was not much to blame, as another man had taken advantage of his extreme poverty to bribe him to commit the crime. It is a curious and interesting point of view. This convict was a very pleasant-looking young fellow, with a frank, open countenance and excellent manners. I will admit that I was glad when I later heard that he was not to be executed.

In the same prison there was a very tiny little Burmese British subject, whom I had met some time before at

Chiengmai. He was caught smuggling opium down to Bangkok by train. The authorities at Chiengmai, having received information after he started on his journey, sent a wire saying: "Search mail train and arrest smallest man on it." This was done, and the opium was found in the smallest man's baggage. The moral seems to be that only people of average stature ought to smuggle opium. It is also a very delicate subject to write or talk about in Siam. A very usual method is to bribe the servants of eminent or ultra-respectable people to conceal opium in their employers' baggage, where its presence is least likely to be suspected. The eminent and respectable people, when the opium happens to be discovered, never can see how funny it is.

The Chiengmai jail is to some extent self-supporting. The prisoners grow flowers and cultivate vegetables; they also breed rabbits; in their workshops they make very good furniture, as well as wicker and rattan articles, such as chairs, baskets and mats. Some of them are occupied in pounding rice for use in the jail or sale outside. This latter is hard work, but they are not kept at it for long at a time. The prisoners look healthy and happy, and seem to regard their warders with friendly feelings, quite devoid of any distrust or hatred.

All illiterate prisoners are taught to read and write, and higher education is provided for those who are already literate. A young professor from the Ministry of Education is attached to the jail, and prisoners who succeed in passing certain examinations are given certificates, the possession of which entitle them to some privileges.

On Sundays, only essential work is done in the jail, and a Buddhist religious service is held for the benefit of the prisoners.

I am sorry I cannot write about all the interesting and amusing people I have met among the inmates of various jails in Siam. Of course, I do not mean to imply that all "criminals", whether in or out of jail, are interesting and amusing. To me it always seems that the inhabitants of a prison are much like any other collection of men and women; they are just a mixture, good, bad and indifferent. There are in fact very few people, in or out of jail, who are entitled to be considered either very good or very bad. I ought, perhaps, to know something about it, for, during the Second World War, I was myself locked up in a prison camp for three years and three months. Maybe, this is why I have a sort of fellow-feeling for convicts, and always feel at my ease among them.

V

Marriage Tangles

"Our father and mother," was the term often applied to the British Consul by Indian and Burmese British subjects in the old days. And they certainly never hesitated to bring all their family and matrimonial troubles along to the Consul for paternal advice.

"You are my father and mother," said to me once a young Pathan from the North-West Frontier Province of India—now in Pakistan—"but you are asking too much of me. I cannot live with a woman who has no legs!" An old couple had appealed to me for help, saying that Nabab, the young Pathan referred to, had married their daughter and deserted her a few months later. When I told him that it was his duty to support his wife, he answered me by saying that she had no legs, and then proceeded to relate the following strange story.

Nabab, it appeared, had recently arrived from India. One day he went for a walk with a friend, when he saw, seated in the verandah of a certain house, a pretty Lao girl, to whom he instantly took a great fancy. She was seated on the floor, and, as it was a cold day, was wrapped in a large shawl, the ends of which were spread around her. Nabab wasted no time, but sent along his friend the next day to make a matrimonial offer to the damsel's parents. The old people only demanded a very moderate sum for their daughter, so terms were easily arranged, and a day was fixed for the wedding.

Nabab, who was a Mahomedan, attended at the proper time, accompanied by a Moulvi and several friends. Prayers were

Blue Meo chieftain.
Photo: Gordon Young

BELOW: Mrabri, also called "Spirits of the Yellow Leaves", whose very existence was doubted until recent years.
Photo: by courtesy of the Siam Society

Lisu girls in New Year's dress.

Lisu boys dressed for courtship. Special seasons and places are
appointed for courtship. *Photo: Gordon Young*

Lahu Nyi chieftain's daughter.   A young Yao girl.

Akha maidens dancing.

Shellen Lahu with gourd pipe, The sound is not unlike that of bagpipes.
Photo: Gordon Young

recited, and the Moulvi pronounced Nabab and the lady of his choice to be man and wife. During the whole proceedings, the bride remained seated on a mat, enveloped in a rug from the waist downwards.

After the ceremony, Nabab and his friends repaired to the Moulvi's house for a "stag party", while the bride's parents said they would prepare the bridal chamber, and instructed Nabab to return at ten o'clock. On the stroke of ten he was there, and was conducted by his parents-in-law to the bridal chamber. A very few moments later, he burst out of the room and angrily denounced the old couple, saying that they had cheated him into marrying a girl with no legs!

The charge was a true one. The bride had no legs. She had feet, but they grew straight out from her body with no intervening limbs. She could, it seems, walk about with the aid of a stick, and even, in case of emergency, was able to creep up and down stairs—but she had no legs!

The bride's parents indignantly denied that they had practised any deceit, protesting that they had never, either verbally or in writing, asserted that their daughter had any legs.

"That may be so," replied Nabab, "but it was your duty to tell me."

"Nonsense!" said the old couple, "if people have a daughter who happens to possess some little defect, a mole, a wart, no legs, or some such trifle, it is not their duty to go about proclaiming and advertising it. Our daughter, it is true, has no legs, but she is absolutely complete in every other respect, and no sensible man would make a fuss about a paltry matter such as a mere lack of legs. In fact, a legless wife is the ideal wife; she cannot spend her time gadding about after other fellows."

To cut a long story short, Nabab allowed himself, in the end, to be persuaded by the specious arguments of his parents-in-law, and to remain with his wife, even though she had no legs.

Not long afterwards it became apparent that although, as biologists would tell us, the lady's leg genes were recessive, her fertility genes were dominant. This was more than Nabab could bear. The sight of his wife, legless but pregnant, was too much for him. He cleared out, and then it was that the old people came to complain to me.

The unfortunate young woman who was the cause of all the trouble was brought for me to inspect, and after I had gazed upon her I decided that it was impossible to ask Nabab, or any man on earth, to continue to live with her. I spoke strongly to Nabab as to his folly in marrying a girl without even knowing whether she had any legs, and his still greater folly in consenting to live with her after he had discovered her limbless condition. "However," I said, "you are responsible for her being pregnant, and you must pay ten ticals a month for her support; moreover, this sum will have to be increased when her child is born."

Nabab paid up for the next few months. Then, without telling anyone, he boarded a train for Bangkok, and from there took the next steamer back to India. He never returned to Siam, and I do not know what happened to him. However, his brief sojourn in Siam was not wasted, for his wife gave birth to twins! I saw them many years later, when they were called up for service in the Siamese army. They were smart, sturdy young fellows, each provided with an excellent pair of very muscular legs.

* * *

Another Mahomedan British subject once came to me to ask my assistance in straightening out a curious marriage tangle. He had, he said, exchanged his buffalo for another man's wife, and now wanted to wriggle out of the bargain.

It appeared that this man, whom we will call Abdul, had no wife, but owned a buffalo, which had been given him in settlement of a bad debt; he had, however, no field for the buffalo to plough. A friend of his—let us call him Ali—had a wife and a field, but no buffalo. So Abdul went to Ali and suggested trading the wife for the buffalo, pointing out the great advantage to a man who owned a field of acquiring a buffalo, as compared with the comparative uselessness of a wife. Ali agreed, and a formal contract was drawn up and signed in the presence of several highly respectable witnesses.

If we disregard the moral aspect of this bargain, but concentrate on its purely practical side, it would seem as though both parties ought to have been satisfied. The bachelor got a wife, and the landowner got a buffalo. However, things did not work out that way at all. Ali who got the buffalo, made no complaint, but Abdul, who acquired the wife, had quite a lot to say. Needless to relate, he came to say it to me, and to beseech me to declare the contract null and void.

I told Abdul that, as an Englishman and a Christian, I regarded the exchange of a wife for a buffalo as a shameful and shocking proceeding, but I pointed out that, as he himself had suggested the deal, and as the other man was satisfied, it ill became him to re-open the matter.

"But, Sir," said Abdul, "you have failed to grasp an essential point. The buffalo cannot talk, but the wife can, and not only can, but does; and moreover, her whole conversation consists in abusing me. It was the plain duty of Ali to warn me that his wife was a non-stop nagger!"

In the end, I agreed to investigate the case, and in due course the two husbands and the wife were all assembled in my office—with the buffalo tethered outside.

After hearing what the two men had to say, I informed them that the whole business was illegal, but I again told Abdul that, as he was the originator of the plan, I would not interfere on his behalf. "And, anyhow," I added, "it is absurd for a great strong chap like you to make such a fuss about a few sharp words from a little woman like that. You ought to be able to control her."

At this point the lady, who up till then had not said much, started to show what she could do.

"Control me," she cried, "just let me see him try it! A worm like Abdul cannot manage me, and I defy any man on earth to do so." She then went on to abuse both her husbands with extraordinary vigour, said a few rather harsh things about the buffalo, and finally turned her attention to me.

I will not defile my pen by repeating what she said about me; all I will mention is that she was extremely fortunate in two respects; (a) that I was not the prophet Elisha, and (b) that there were no bears in the neighbourhood.

In the end she was escorted, still talking, to a rickshaw, and my last recollection of her is her voice, which could be heard for some time after the rickshaw had turned the corner and was out of sight

I agreed with both the husbands in preferring the buffalo, which had done nothing but quietly chew the cud throughout the proceedings.

* * *

I was once dining in the house of a Danish police officer in the Siamese service when suddenly a young Hindu, whom I knew slightly, named Ram Das, walked into the room, saluted my Danish friend, and calmly announced: "I have come to report that I have just cut off my wife's nose. Here is the nose, and here is the knife."

He then plonked down on the dining-table a blood-stained knife and an unpleasant object which proved, on investigation, to be a human nose and part of an upper lip.

My Danish friend popped the nose into a glass of whisky, and promptly arrested the visitor, who in due course was brought up before the local Siamese Court.

Rain Das seemed quite unable to realise that he had done anything wrong. In India, at that time, women were kept in seclusion, but in Siam they are almost as free as their sisters in England or America. His Lao wife, it appeared, had annoyed him by talking and joking with a young male cousin of hers, and when remonstrances had failed to cure her of this shocking habit, her husband cut off her nose. And why shouldn't he?

His advocate put up a two-fold defence. Firstly, it was claimed, Ram Das had committed no offence at all, since under the ancient Siamese law of husband and wife, promulgated in A.D. 1359, a husband is permitted to inflict proper and suitable punishment on his wife if she misbehaves herself. Secondly, the whole affair was an accident. Ram Das only intended to cut off the tip of his wife's nose; she, however, instead of staying still while he did this, as it was her obvious duty to do, resisted and struggled; she thus caused his hand to slip, and he accidentally cut off the whole of her nose and part of her lip.

The Court was not impressed by these arguments, and sent Ram Das to jail for eight years. While in jail, he wrote and sent to me a beautiful poem, giving an account of his whole life, down to and including the nose episode. He also wrote some touching verses addressed to his wife, enjoining her to wait for him and to remain faithful. I do not know whether she did so, but judging from her appearance, with no nose and only half a lip, I should say it would have been difficult for the poor woman to do otherwise.

A British "father and mother" in bygone times in Siam often found the ways of his polyglot children hard to fathom. Now they have Consuls of their own race. Will they meet with greater sympathy and understanding? I wonder.

VI

Foreign Courts and Colleagues

The Siamese authorities sometimes complained, and with good cause, of the fact that, though most foreign powers exercised jurisdiction over their own nationals—and some powers interpreted the word *subject* or *protégé* in a very liberal sense—yet few foreign Consuls were provided with any proper machinery for carrying out their jurisdiction.

In fact, the British and French Consular Courts were the only ones which functioned in a methodical manner, or which possessed any proper jail accommodation. A certain other smaller power had a tiny jail, but I only ever heard of one convict languishing therein, and he only languished from 2 till 11 p.m. on the day of his conviction, and then drove away in a carriage and pair and was never seen again.

It was really quite an undertaking to attempt to secure adequate punishment for serious foreign malefactors, unless they happened to be British or French subjects. Nobody even supposed that the United States, German, Italian or Portuguese Consular Court would, say, execute a man for murder, or keep him locked up for more than a few days. In fact, if they were forced to convict one of their subjects or citizens they usually asked the British Consul for the loan of a cell in the British Consular jail.

I must admit that the lack of a handy jail rather cramps a Consul's judicial style in dealing with criminals, great or small. I felt this myself when I ran a Consular Court at Singora.

A foreign Consul would now and then burst into the British Consulate-General in a frenzy of excitement because one of his nationals happened to have been charged with theft or assault, and would enquire if things like this ever happened in regard to British subjects, and if so, what we did about it. I, a lad in my early twenties, would calm the poor old colleague down, and would explain that I had myself tried a dozen or so similar cases that very day, and that it was not really so frightfully difficult as it looked. He would be greatly comforted, especially after I had assured him that, if he could bring himself up to the pitch of convicting his man, we would try to find a cosy nook for the prisoner in our jail at extremely reasonable rates.

One foreigner who was thus accommodated in our jail wrote and complained about it to Lord Salisbury. His contention was that he was an innocent man, and that we knew it; we ought therefore to have refused to connive at an injustice by lending a cell for him to be put into. As a matter of fact we really did believe that he was innocent, but as every foreign Consul had been accustomed to expect our assistance in this kind of matter for forty years, we could hardly impugn the justice of the Consul concerned by refusing to receive his convict, especially as our jail was almost empty at the time.

What happened was this. The prisoner, X., who ran a small hotel, had some time before written to complain to the Foreign Minister of his country that his Consul was collecting certain illegal fees. The Consul received a rap over the knuckles, and thereafter lay in wait for X.'s blood. Some months later, a guest at the hotel left without paying his bill, and X. detained a guitar belonging to him. He complained to the Consul, who sent for X. and asked him: "Is it true that you have kept Mr. B.'s guitar without his consent?" On X.'s admitting this, the Consul, filled with glee, at once said:

"You have pleaded guilty to the charge of stealing a guitar. I sentence you to one year's imprisonment."

It was very amusing, but X. could not see the joke. However, as we refused to keep him for more than a fortnight, he was sent by his Consul to one of his country's colonies, the Governor of which immediately quashed the sentence and sent him back to Bangkok. There he remained, and devised all kinds of ingenious methods of worrying his Consul.

I recollect that X., after his arrest, tried to induce us to register him as a British subject, and a fair number of other foreigners who had taken a dislike to their own Consuls made the same attempt. They were always very surprised when we turned them down, and seemed to think that they had just as much right to be British subjects as whatever it was that they were supposed to be. Sometimes they had.

If relations between the British Consulate and some foreign Consulate happened to be strained, as sometimes occurred on account of delicate questions of official precedence or other such ticklish matters, it was a splendid opportunity for the disgruntled Consul's nationals to crack one another on the head. The Consul was not going to ask us for the loan of a cell, and as he himself had nowhere to keep prisoners, the accused was certain to get off with a fine.

I only once appeared in a foreign Consular Court, and that was to prosecute a young ruffian for stealing my harness. He was seen walking out of the gate of the British Legation carrying the harness, and he sold it the same day to a pawn-broker, who identified him. Nevertheless, he was acquitted, on the ground that he had not actually been seen removing the harness from the stable. He might, therefore, have acquired it by honest means somewhere between the stable and the front gate, and must be given the benefit of the doubt. I told the foreign Consul who delivered this judgment that I thought he was wrong, which annoyed him intensely. Two months later he came up to me at a garden party and informed me that he had submitted the case to his father, who was a celebrated jurist, and that his father had said he was quite right. In reply, I asked him what his grandmother had said about it. This made him really angry, and he complained to the British Minister that I had insulted him. As he was about forty years older than I, maybe I was a bit cheeky. Anyhow, I wrote him a nice apology, saying that I was not really interested in what his grandmother thought about his judgment.

When foreign witnesses were wanted in our Court, it was quite a business collecting them, as each one had to be summoned through his own Consul. On one occasion I wrote a letter to a foreign Consul asking him to be good enough to procure the attendance of one of his *protégés* in the case of *Regina* versus *Z*. My colleague replied as follows: "I shall have much pleasure in arranging for the attendance of the witness required, but there is a fee of five ticals for issuing the summons. Will you kindly request the plaintiff, Mr. Regina, to call at my office and pay the fee."

Regina paid the fee, but not in person.

The British Consul was often asked to take charge of foreign Consulates and their Courts. I have an impression that the subjects of the foreign powers concerned did not, as a rule, much like us; I remember that some foreign subjects whom the British Consul thought it desirable to send to jail complained that their own Consul never treated them in so coarse a manner.

On different occasions we were in charge of the Danish, Portuguese and Italian Consulates.

When we were in charge of the Danish Consulate, C. once came upon a Dane and an Englishman fighting fiercely on a bridge over a muddy canal near the Legation. Realising that whichever side won we were in for trouble, he tried to stop them, but failing, hurried along to call the Consul. When the Consul came on the scene, only the Dane was visible, seated in solitary state in the soft mud at the side of the canal. "Where is Simpson?" called out the Consul. "Here," replied the Viking, raising himself in the mud, and then sitting down again with great emphasis. The Consul and C. were pretty muddy by the time they had settled that dispute.

About the same time as the canal episode, another Dane challenged another Englishman to a duel with pistols—to the death! Late at night the Dane came along to see the British

Consul. "Mr. Consul," said he, "Jones and I are fighting a duel—to the death—at Sapatoom tomorrow morning at six. Nothing will deter us, so it would be useless for you to try to do so. However, as we are both under your protection, I mention the matter to you, in order that you may make preparations for the funeral of one or both of us."

Hardly had he crept out, when the Englishman came along with the same tale. Quite useless, he said, to try to interfere, but he thought it only fair to let the Consul know about the matter, in case he might like to make some pretence of objecting, in order to save his face.

The two combatants duly betook themselves to Sapatoom at six the next morning, and were both of them unspeakably surprised to find the British Consul there ahead of them, accompanied by a dozen Siamese policemen.

I was myself once challenged to fight a duel by a fire-eating subject of a certain power for which I happened at the time to be acting as Consul. This gentleman was collecting money for some alleged charity, and when I asked to see his credentials, he accused me of insulting him, and demanded satisfaction. I replied that I was unversed in the etiquette of duelling, but understood that, as the challenged party, I had the right to choose the weapons. I therefore chose Gillette razors, which were the only weapons I had been trained to use.

This gentleman, I must confess, treated me more courteously than one of my own compatriots whom, at about the same time, I had occasion to fine five ticals for being drunk and disorderly. Without issuing any challenge whatever, he took off his boots and threw them at my head. Luckily for me, he was a bad shot, but it rather annoyed me at the time, all the same.

There used often to be fearful jealousy and hate in the Diplomatic and Consular Corps over questions of precedence. We Britishers were as bad as anyone else. Among the juniors the rank of Consular Assistant was the cause of much heart-burning. A First or Second Assistant in the British Consulate-General was often a man of several years' service, and it annoyed him to be put behind some foreigner who had just arrived in the country, but bore the rank of Vice-Consul. This is not the case now, as British Consular Officers are given the rank of Vice-Consul after their period of probation.

Perhaps we got on better with the Siamese than did some of our foreign colleagues. I remember one elderly foreign diplomat rushing into the British Minister's office, pale with fury, and maintaining that the Siamese Foreign Minister had insulted him. "Le vieux farceur vient de me faire une tête." I am sure that the then Foreign Minister, the late Prince Devawongse Varoprakar, who was one of the pleasantest and politest of men, never made a "tête" at anyone; but however that may be, the poor old diplomat had to be plied with brandy—lots of it—before he felt better.

One German Minister had a rather trying experience. He used to drive a dog-cart, somewhat unskilfully, and one day managed to knock down a Chinaman just outside the Sam-Yek police station. The police ran out and arrested him, and as there was nobody present who could speak English, much less German, and as he was too infuriated to be intelligible in any language, he remained there for some time. At last a passing Englishman, seeing that something was up, went in and rescued him, explaining to the police that they had collared a foreign Minister, and had better let him go.

Berlin was much incensed, and demanded a public apology which was duly given some weeks later. A German flag was run up in front of the police station where the outrage had been committed, the Chief of Police read an apology, the Minister—described in the local Press as a pale but dignified figure—replied, a brass band played the German National Anthem, and the German Government was satisfied that a very salutary impression had been created on the populace.

Maybe the German Government was mistaken. Anyhow, my Siamese boy brought me my tea late that afternoon, and explained to me, by way of excuse for his unpunctuality: "I could not get back in time, Sir, owing to the large crowd which was watching a most interesting ceremony at Sam-Yek. The German Minister got drunk some weeks ago, and ran over a Chinaman with his dog-cart; today he was making a public apology to the King of Siam for his evil behaviour. Afterwards, a band played "God save the Queen" as a mark of respect to the British Minister, because *he* never behaves in such a vulgar manner."

Some of the most charming and pleasant diplomatic and consular people I ever met were the Japanese. N., one of the earliest Japanese Consuls in Siam, was a very popular figure. I remember once at dinner hearing an Englishman holding forth on that stale and dubious old theory of the worthlessness and unreliability of all "native Christians". Finally, he turned to N. and asked him: "How about Japan? Do you not find that all your native Christians come from the dregs of society, and are despised and distrusted by every respectable Japanese?" "Well," replied N., "my opinion is perhaps just a little biased. You see, I am myself one of those native Christians."

Another time, when N. was dining with me, the servant accidentally poured some hot soup down his neck. When I apologised, he exclaimed: "Ah, but I like it! It is what I call *snog* and *cawzee!*"

As I mentioned above, certain foreign representatives were inclined to apply for British advice when faced with an emergency. Once, when a certain power suddenly changed its form of government, a distracted Minister rushed in to ask his British colleague what was the proper thing to do under such circumstances. The Briton replied that he found it hard to advise him, as he himself never had been, and never expected to be, in a like position. "But," persisted the other, "just suppose that the King of England were to be turned out, you *must* know what you would do. Would you resign or not?" "Yes, then; in the improbable case that you mention, I would resign at once." "Thank you so much. I am sure you are right." However, he changed his mind when he got home, set his wife to work on a new flag, sat up late typing revised headings on his official stationery, and faced the world next morning in quite a new capacity.

Though it is easy to see the quaint side of an episode of this kind, it is perhaps not very clear what is a man's duty in the circumstances referred to. By resigning, he might cause a great deal of inconvenience to his fellow countrymen, besides possibly forfeiting his pay and pension, and if a man has a family and is not well off he can hardly be blamed for hesitating to make a martyr of himself. Personally, I should counsel a discreet delay. The change of régime might, after all, prove not to be permanent.

The United States Minister, when I first came to Siam, was the Hon. J. B., one of the most generous and warmhearted men I ever met, and *some* orator. He had a famous story, which was published in several American papers, of how his Chinese cook was found dead on the floor of the kitchen one Christmas night, and how all the guests stood round the corpse and sang "Auld Lang Syne". Like so much good fiction, this story had a substantial basis of fact, for Mr. B.'s cook really was taken ill with cholera one Christmas night, when he had a number of guests to dinner, and died shortly afterwards.

But in those days one did not pay much attention to cholera corpses—they were so commonplace.

There used to be a certain foreign Consul in Bangkok who always looked rather grubby and untidy. One day, at an official function, he was observed to have a button missing from his uniform, and a bluff British colleague asked him why he didn't sew on a new one. He explained that he had no spare buttons, but had written home for one. "Well, you are all covered with medals," replied the Briton, "why don't you hang one of them over the button-hole. It looks awful as it is."

Sure enough, at the next official function, our friend *did* hang a large medal over the button-hole. This time, the American Minister wanted to know why he wore a medal on the middle of his stomach. "Well," replied he, "I got that for services rendered to the Ministry of the Interior."

This reminds me of a British Consul who once left his uniform hanging over a chair while he was dressing, and found that his bull terrier pup had chewed all the embroidery off the sleeves. He then put it on, lest worse might befall it, and proceeded to shave. He cut his chin, smeared soap all over his shoulders, and arrived at the Palace late, with lacerated chin, soapy shoulders, and chewed embroidery. The date happened to be 4th November, and when he nervously asked the British Minister whether he was late, the latter testily replied: "No, you are a day too early. Tomorrow is Guy Fawkes' Day."

This same Consul, who was always a bit careless in his dress, on another occasion was attending a royal garden party, at which, in those days, frock coats were worn. He discovered, at the last moment, that cockroaches had eaten two large holes in his only available pair of trousers. "No matter," said his wife, "the holes are well above the level of the bottom of the frock coat. Keep it buttoned, and all will be well."

It was a hot day, and the Consul soon forgot his wife's sage advice, and stood for some time conversing with a Very Exalted Personage, having flung his frock coat open, thereby displaying two large expanses of white shirt peeping through the holes in his trousers, to the huge delight of all beholders, except the British Minister, who nearly fainted with rage.

Looking back, I realise that the members of the Diplomatic and Consular Corps in Bangkok, when I first made my debut, were a remarkable body of men. When they all assembled at the Palace on the King of Siam's birthday, resplendent in every sort of garb, uniform and otherwise, and a marvellous variety of headgear—cocked hats, top hats, peaked caps, pickelhaubes and other unclassified lids—I wonder what His Majesty really thought about them. Maybe he found them rather amusing. I did, anyhow.

VII

Some Amusements

Siamese and Lao boxing differs quite a lot from ours. The feet may be used, and are used by some boxers to excess, and there is a certain amount of semi-wrestling, semi-jujutsu work. I am told that eighty-four different varieties of punch, grab, shove and kick are recognised; if a boxer tries to introduce an eighty-fifth kind, he is guilty of a foul. For instance, it is a foul to hold your opponent's head under your arm and thump it, or to jump on his face after knocking him down.

One curious coup which I have seen is what I call the wheelbarrow stroke. One man suddenly seizes the other by the leg and pushes him backwards as hard as he can against the rope. It does not seem to do much good, but it pleases the audience; and, after all, that is what boxing is for.

Some boxers are very quick with their feet. I have seen a man get in a proper right and left in this way.

A Siamese or Lao boxer, before beginning to fight, often goes through various genuflections, kneeling on the ground and raising his hands in honour of his "teacher". After that he may do a little dancing. Sometimes the two opponents dance round each other for quite a long time before they get down to business. Some of them dance very well, and when knocked down will get up again not only smiling, but dancing. They almost always show the greatest good humour throughout the fight, and will smile and joke as long as they are able to stand up.

I like the Lao boxers. They may not be scientific from the Western point of view, but they have plenty of pluck, and are always full of fun.

In the Siamese Peninsular States the people are very fond of bull-fighting. Bull against bull, be it understood. To us these fights seem rather tame affairs. In nine cases out of ten the fight consists merely in a trial of strength, one bull pushing against the other with its head, until the weaker of the combatants is forced back, when it turns and runs. The victor rarely pursues the vanquished for more than a few yards, and it is unusual for either of them to suffer very severe injuries. Sometimes their heads are a bit gory, but that is about all.

The runaway bull is brought back for a second round, but as a rule he is not having any, and if he does it is a half-hearted affair, and does not last long; though on one occasion I saw a bull, beaten in the first round, which came back for a second round, fought for over half an hour, routed his rival, chased him from the ring, followed him into the street, knocked him down and gored him in the stomach. He then finished up by knocking down a Chinaman and goring him in the stomach too. It was the most exciting bull-fight I ever saw, and everybody enjoyed it except the Chinaman.

It cannot be said that Siamese bull-fights, as a rule, are very brutal or degrading spectacles.

Some fighting bulls are very fierce, so to speak, in private life. When we lived at Singora, a neighbour's fighting bull broke into our compound and severely gored one of our ponies. But he got as good as he gave, for a tiny little pet pony of my wife's, about eight hands high, joined in the fray, seized the bull by the tail, and would not let go until he had almost chewed it off. After that, the owner of the bull wanted to sue me for damages.

The legal point here involved reminds me of the case of a friend of mine whose car collided with a cyclist. The latter, after receiving hospital treatment, went round to see my friend, accompanied by a lawyer, and threatened to claim enormous damages. My friend, who had been making enquiries, propounded the following five queries to the claimant:

1. Are you almost blind?
2. Have you recently been confined in a lunatic asylum?
3. Were you drunk when the accident occurred?
4. Was it your first attempt to ride a bicycle?
5. Had you stolen the bicycle?

The answers to all five questions were in the affirmative. The claim fell through.

To return to fighting beasts. In the State of Patani the people keep fighting rams, which may fairly be called battering rams. The animals are launched at one another from a distance of several yards, and charge head on with tremendous force, the impact producing a sound which can be heard all over the neighbourhood. The rams then draw back and charge again, and so on until one of them is too exhausted to keep it up any longer. It seems marvellous that their skulls are not cracked open; they must be extremely thick.

Siamese fighting fish are well known. They are very beautiful little creatures, with long, lacy fins, and their scales show all the colours of a sunset sky. Their pugnacity is remarkable; not infrequently both combatants succumb to their injuries, their fins being so torn that they cannot swim. A great deal of money is often staked on fish fights, but to foreigners they are more or less slow and unexciting performances. Sometimes the two fishes will hold on to one another's mouths for almost an hour; the spectators wait in a state of rapt attention, but I must admit that I have often longed to poke the performers with a stick to liven them up a bit. I have often felt the same at a cricket match.

Cock-fighting is very popular, but this is, of course, nothing peculiar to Siam. Cricket fighting I have never seen, but I claim to be an expert at beetle fighting, having once kept a stable of five rhinoceros beetles, all tethered to sticks of sugar cane. To tether a beetle, all you have to do is to drive a post—a match will serve—into your sugar cane, and attach the beetle's horn to the post by a piece of string, leaving it to graze contentedly on the cane.

A rhinoceros beetle has two horns, one on its head, where a horn ought to be, and one in the middle of its thorax. The thorax horn is stationary, and the insect bites by bringing its head horn into contact with its thorax horn.

Just as some male elephants have only rudimentary tusks, so also some rhinoceros beetles are only provided with miserable, useless little horns on their backs, which are quite unable to nip anything, being too short to meet with the head horns. It is very mysterious why Nature should thus pick and choose in distributing her gifts among elephants and beetles. It is true that some men cannot grow whiskers; but then, after all, whiskers are not, like tusks and horns, of any use in a fight. Quite the other way, in fact.

This is how beetles are made to fight. A long stick is prepared, in the middle of which there is a little, scooped-out prison chamber, shut by a tiny door, and containing an even tinier window. In this little prison a lady beetle is placed, unapproachable, yet partly visible, and presumably smell-able. The two fighters are put on to the stick, and they fight for the lady. They are not always very keen, and have to be led on by the use of little tin buzzers on sticks, which are twiddled near them in order to excite them. They rarely, if ever, inflict any visible wounds on one another, but when their bodies are well pinched they give forth a curious hissing noise, which rather gives one the idea that they are feeling uncomfortable. Their owners revive them, between the rounds, by spitting sugar-cane juice on to them, and sometimes by fanning them. If one of the beetles runs away, and will not come back, he is adjudged the loser. Sometimes, too, one of the beetles will seize the other with his horns, drag him by force off the stick, and heave him bodily forth into the wide world.

The lady beetle has, I always think, a very thin time, cooped up in her tiny cell, while her rival lovers fight above her skylight window. Neither victor nor vanquished is for her, anyhow, for love-making is held to be extremely bad for fighting beetles. A lot of money is staked on these fights, and the owner of a first class beetle may make quite large sums out of it. But the poor beetle, after all its fighting, is not even allowed to snatch a hasty kiss. I call this unjust.

When I owned fighting beetles, I always set the female free after the battle, and let her fly away with the victor. Off they went, and never came back any more, and everybody thought me a sentimental fool.

To catch new fighting beetles, all that is necessary is to hang out a stick of sugar cane in the verandah at night. In the morning there will often be one or more beetles browsing on the cane. You just slip a noose over their horns, and there you are.

In former times, people used to race tortoises, urging them on to unnatural rates of speed by kindling fires on their backs. The Siamese Government long ago prohibited this cruel sport, but nevertheless I once saw such a race. It was in a distant jungle village near Pailin, and the promoters, I blush to say, were British subjects. I came on them unexpectedly, late at night, and remember the scene well. A couple of dozen excited men, brandishing torches in a bamboo thicket, and in their midst two wretched tortoises, running frantically with some horrible resinous substance flaring on their backs. It was a most devilish thing, and yet I do not think anyone there realised bow cruel it was. I rushed in, seized one of the tortoises and threw mud and sand on its shell, and the meeting broke up in confusion. The tortoise I dealt with was not much damaged, but the other one, which I caught later on, had to be killed.

These tortoise hunters were very backward and uncouth people. They did not even have the decency to wear green uniforms with brass buttons when they set forth to bait defenceless creatures to death, as is customary with civilised sportsmen. For instance, English otter hunters.

The Siamese have some kinds of foot races which are very amusing. Their relay race is run by two teams of six or eight men each. The course is marked by a long rope, at each end of which the opposing teams take their places. The two first men start towards each other, running on opposite sides of the rope, each holding a flag. They run right round the rope, handing the flag to the next member of their team, who repeats the performance. This continues until a member of one team catches up his opponent and touches him on the back with his flag. If the teams are well matched, they may go on running until they are all exhausted. I have run in many of these relay races, and found them very good sport. Often one side has almost won, when the flag passes to a faster member of the opposing team, and the position may in a short time be quite reversed. This kind of race is called in Siamese *Wing Piow*.

Sack races are much funnier in Siam than in the West. The competitors are put bodily into the sacks, heads and all, and the mouth of the sack is then tied up. They may proceed in any way they like, but the favourite method is by rolling along the ground. If they roll off the course, their backers are allowed to shove them back. It is rather a heating affair.

The Siamese are extremely fond of the theatre. Of late years all kinds of Western innovations have been introduced on to the Siamese stage, and it is fashionable to regret this, and to bewail the decay of the old "classical" traditions; but I, for one, much prefer the more lively methods of modern days, for I must admit that I found the old style of Siamese classical drama almost insufferably boring. I could only bear it at all if I was allowed to doze through the performance, but I was seldom left to slumber, kindly disposed friends always insisting on waking me up and explaining the plot to me. On one occasion I had changed my seat three times, so as to escape from plot-explainers, and at last came to anchor between two American Reverends, feeling confident that I would be safe there. Not a bit of it! Hardly had I dozed off when they jointly woke me up and started to explain the plot to me. I may add that the play was one which no clergyman ought to have attended without first stuffing his ears with sterilised cotton wool.

In the classical dramas, or *Lakhons,* all the players, except a few comic characters, were women, and the acting tended to be conventional, and made no attempt to "hold the mirror up to Nature". The comic plays, or *Yiké,* were much more amusing. All the performers were men, and there was a good deal of slap-stick farce, and a good deal of extremely broad humour. At the present time there are many *Yiké* theatres in which both men and women take part. The actors and actresses are often remarkably clever at improvising verses, one capping the other, and trying to outdo him or her in audacity.

I once saw a comic funeral scene performed in a village theatre. One actor, dressed like a bishop, wearing a huge mitre, and carrying an enormous book, walked at the head of the procession, saying at intervals, "Goddam, Goddam!" I asked the man next me what sort of a bishop it was, and he slyly assured me that it was an English bishop, because French bishops never say "Goddam". However, I explained to him that Anglican bishops only say "Goddam" when playing golf; never when conducting funerals.

The Siamese and Laos, when freed from the restrictions of their classic drama, are very good actors. King Rama VI who died in 1925, was a keen supporter of the theatre, and himself wrote a number of plays of the modern type, besides translating or adapting several foreign plays for the Siamese stage, including three of Shakespeare's. King Rama's plays are good, and I have derived much enjoyment from seeing some of them acted.

As for Shakespeare, I do not think it is possible to translate his plays into Siamese without losing their whole spirit—the genius of the two languages is too different. In fact, Shakespeare is only translatable into the Teutonic or Scandinavian languages. In German, Shakespeare may be quite good, but in Italian he is poor stuff, and in French perfectly horrible.

The Malays are very fond of Shakespeare, but they do not do much more than use his plots—there is no serious attempt made at translation. They usually act his plays, tragedies as well as comedies, as comic operettas, with songs and dances thrown in, most of the tunes being English popular airs of many years ago. They do not like important events to take place off-stage. For instance, in *Hamlet* they will not allow Ophelia to sneak away and drown herself on the sly, thus cheating the audience, who have paid to see the whole story, so she has to kill herself on the stage. When I saw it acted, she shot herself in the stomach with a revolver, to the tune of "Her golden hair was hanging down her back". I understand that in another version of the play she emulates Cleopatra by letting a large cobra bite her, to the tune of "The honeysuckle and the bee".

The Siamese National Anthem is a very fine piece of music. It is said to have been composed for King Narai of Siam by the band-master of Louis XIV, and certainly there is something about it which is not distinctively Siamese. Its chief fault is that it is a bit too long, a fault which it shares with the "Star-spangled Banner". There is also a new national song, introduced after Siam became a Constitutional Monarchy in 1934. This also is a very fine piece of music, and lends itself better to hearty singing by large numbers of men than is the case with the old anthem.

The present King of Siam, Bhumibol Adulyadej, is a very gifted composer, and has produced a number of patriotic marches.

In Siam, everybody stands up in a respectful manner when their National Anthem is played, which is a very pleasant thing to see. In England, we also tend to treat "God Save the Queen" with proper respect; but in cinemas in some parts of the British Empire I have been shocked to hear only two or three bars rattled out at the end of the performance, the audience meanwhile getting ready to go out without paying the slightest attention to it.

Talking of cinemas makes me think of the Chiengmai cinemas thirty or more years ago. No film less than ten years old was ever shown, and most of the films had come to pieces and been stuck together again—all wrong. There was a famous film called the *Hypnotic Detective,* in which the sleuth started

by hauling the criminal off to jail for a murder which one saw
being committed an hour later. Some of the films would have
failed to pass the Censor at home. One of these, called
Father's Purge, was extremely popular.

A curious thing about the Chiengmai cinemas was, and still
is, that a number of young fellows derive great satisfaction
from standing, night after night, *outside* a cinema hall. Many
of them never go in to see the show, and so far as I can make
out they are not usually in search of amorous adventures—
I mean to say, not more than everybody always is. They
themselves seem unable to explain why they go there beyond
saying that it is *muan* (jolly). We formerly had a chauffeur
who, when not on duty, stood in front of a cinema hall as
regular as clockwork, from eight till eleven every night,
wearing a saxe blue blazer with brass buttons. I dare say he is
standing there now.

VIII

Oddities

I have no intention of trying to give a systematic account of Siamese and Lao folklore or curious beliefs. All I propose to do is to describe a few odd things which I have met with from time to time.

Siamese medicine, as it existed before the introduction of Western ideas, was by no means an art to be despised. There were, and are, a large number of Siamese and Lao remedies of very great value. A Siamese doctor, untrained in modern medical science, has been known to cure cases of cholera which appeared quite hopeless, and for various skin diseases and internal complaints they have some very efficacious drugs. I was once cured of a bad cold by blowing a Siamese remedy up my nose through a silver tube. This caused me to lie on my bed sneezing, without intermission, for three and a half hours. At the end of that time I was so weak that I had to get my servant to support me when I tried to get up; but the cold had vanished. I never used this remedy again.

Siamese indigenous medicine is based on the theory that the human body is composed of the four elements, fire, earth, air or wind and water. When the proper proportion of these elements is disturbed, illness results. In practice, it is almost always the wind, or *lom,* which goes wrong. *Lom* is the commonest of all diseases in Siam, and must be responsible for a very large proportion of all the deaths in the kingdom. *Lom,* be it clearly understood, has nothing whatever to do with flatulence. It is a mysterious condition which no foreigner has ever quite succeeded in understanding. Very often people who seem to us to be suffering from quite ordinary complaints, such as malaria or influenza, are said to be afflicted with *lom*, and many patients have assured me, when they were recovering, that they could actually feel the wind escaping through the tips of their fingers and toes. Faintness and fits are almost always due to *lom*.

Lom is not merely a popular term, but is officially recognised, and many of the deaths of government officials recorded in the *Government Gazette* are stated to be due to this cause.

I have tried to find out exactly what *lom* really is ever since I first came to Siam, but I have failed.

One English doctor I knew, when he was not quite sure what was the matter with a patient, always told him that he was suffering from *lom*, and as this term seems to include a vast number of pathological conditions, it is a pretty safe thing to diagnose. Anyhow, a doctor who diagnoses *lom* can defy the whole world to prove that he is wrong.

A man I knew, hearing one of his servants groaning, and being told that the man was suffering from *lom*, fell into one of those pitfalls so plentifully provided by the Siamese language. *Lom*, pronounced with a different tone, means to fall down, and my friend understood that the patient had fallen down and hurt himself. Imagining that one of the man's legs looked rather wobbly, he diagnosed compound fracture, and hurriedly set the supposedly damaged limb in a home-made splint. This treatment proved so successful that the next time the servant had a feverish attack he begged his master to tie another bit of wood to his leg.

The idea that what is good for one thing is good for anything is not uncommon. A Chinese British subject was once charged before me with selling adulterated liquor. His defence was that he had only put into the liquor a health-giving medicine for the benefit of his customers. On further enquiry, it appeared that this medicine was a lotion which had been given him for a sore leg. It did his leg so much good that he nobly decided to pour what was left over into his *samshu* for the benefit of his customers—without extra charge.

Massage is much used in Siam, and many of the masseurs

and masseuses are very skilful, and are usually able greatly to ease the pain caused by sprains or strains, as well as to benefit the body when suffering from various internal diseases.

One masseur I recollect whose treatment required, as its finale, that every joint in the body should be made to click. First he clicked my fingers, my elbows, my wrists and my shoulders; then he clicked my toes, ankles, knees and thighs. Lastly, he put a foot on each of my shoulders and made ready to pull my head until my neck clicked. "No," cried I in alarm, "I can't have that! Nobody is ever allowed to click my neck. My head might come off!" The masseur was rather annoyed, and said that I risked rendering the whole performance useless by refusing to have my neck clicked. However, I remained firm, and it is only fair to add that the treatment did me a lot of good, even though my neck was never clicked.

Love potions are widely believed in, especially by country people, and I have often been assured that they are very efficacious.

Once, when my wife and I were camping in a jungle village, an elderly man came to see us, bringing a present of a little fruit and some rice. Many country folk, who have met with some of the American medical missionaries— always ready to treat and dose poor people for nothing— take all foreigners for doctors. It was so in this case. "Doctor," said our visitor, "I am a very poor man, and can pay you little or nothing, but I beseech you to have pity on me. I have been a widower for three years, and am anxious to marry again, but I am so frightfully ugly that none of the women or girls in the village will look at me. I have tried every one of them without success. I know that you foreign doctors possess wonderfully powerful medicines. Give me, I beg you, a potion which will make the girls love me."

I assured him, firstly, that I was not a doctor, and secondly, that foreign doctors did not deal in the sort of drugs he required. He thought that I was merely being mean and hard-hearted, and begged me again, with tears in his eyes, to relent and take pity on him. So I relented at last, and gave him two compound rhubarb and liquorice pills, which I told him to swallow in water at eight o'clock the following morning. We left at six, so were not there to see the result, but I heard later that the old fellow had married a very pretty girl. No doubt it became known that the foreign doctor had given him a magic love potion, and all the girls forthwith began to find attractions in his ugly face which they never had noticed before.

Love potions are said to be sometimes given to their masters by servants, in order to render them more tolerant of their faults, and more inclined to raise their wages whenever asked to do so.

Dr. Reginald Le May, in his delightful book *An Asian Arcady*, relates how a servant of his tried to dose him with some noxious substance in his drinking water, in order to render him more tractable. I knew the boy in question, and meeting him some time later, I told him that Dr. Le May had published an account of his performance. He was rather flattered to learn that his alleged feat had been made known, as he said, "in every region of the earth," but he utterly denied that he had really put anything into his master's drinking water. But he probably did. Anyhow, I happen to know that his mother was a witch.

I was once warned that one of my servants had put a love potion into some fruit which he had given me. I at once said that I would eat the fruit, so as to show how little attention I paid to such matters; but when I was given details of the probable ingredients, I changed my mind, so cannot say from personal experience what effect such charms may have.

There are charms far more dangerous than love potions. A little image of an enemy, made from mud dug out of one of his footprints, and buried at a cross-road with a pin stuck through it, may prove very deadly. This is, of course, nothing peculiarly Siamese. In the reign of James I, Lady Essex, with the aid of the celebrated magician Dr. Forman, tried to get rid of her husband by similar methods. The only one of these images I ever saw was put under a man's house, with a long thorn stuck in its face. The intended victim found it, and was at once afflicted with a frightful twitching of the facial muscles. It took a long time to cure him, and the cure involved a trip to the seaside and the purchase of a very expensive counter-charm.

Protective charms may be found in plenty. The two Siamese characters *khaw* and *ngaw* tattooed on the leg are an absolute safeguard against snake-bite. This I can personally guarantee, for I have them tattooed on my left leg, and have never been bitten by a snake. Other charms may be tattooed on a man's back to protect him against almost every sort of illness or mishap.

Tattooing is of course, the best sort of charm, being impossible to lose. But a little strip of palm-leaf with the necessary formula written on it is often very effective. I know some boxers who never enter the ring without one of these tied on somewhere, usually on the left arm. A poor lad who was killed some tune ago in a boxing match at Chiengmai was wearing one of these charms. But it appears that his opponent had a better one.

Invulnerability! It would be possible to write a biggish book about charms to ward off sword or bullet wounds. There are dozens of different kinds—tattoo marks, written formulas, knotted strings, tiny images of Buddha, precious stones, dried seeds, needles in the body, and others too numerous to mention.

A young policeman was once found dying by the side of a road near Lampang, with a deep knife wound in his side. Before he expired, he gave the following account of what had happened to him: he had recently acquired a very potent amulet to confer invulnerability, which he boastingly showed to a friend, the Assistant District Officer. The latter said:

"Let us test it," and promptly stabbed him with a dagger.

His friend was arrested, but flatly denied the whole story,

and as there was no corroboration of the dying man's statement, the prisoner had to be released. He was, however, transferred to another post, where he shot a man, and was sent to jail for twenty years.

What justification could there be for such an act as stabbing a man in order to test an amulet? None, it would seem, unless the assailant were absolutely convinced of the infallibility of the charm, and such absolute conviction would surely be impossible unless a test had been made. In any case, it is clearly a crime to make the test by stabbing a vital part of the body.

A Shan charm against wounds consists in inserting uncut rubies or sapphires under the skin. These form lumps, which make part of a tattooed pattern, and the theory is that knives or bullets are magically attracted towards one of the gems, against which they strike harmlessly. The precious stones are rarely of any great intrinsic value, but this fact did not save the life of a poor young Shan at Pailin, who was brutally murdered for the sake of the rubies under his skin, which were certainly not worth more than a couple of shillings. It is rather tragic to think that the very charm on which the simple-minded youth relied for protection was the cause of his being cruelly murdered.

Another charm, originally also a Shan one, is often used by Siamese and Laos—usually by rather tough customers. This consists in inserting needles under the skin. The needles travel about in the body, and in time most of them work their way to the surface. Some of them form a small ulcer and come out, but others remain for years just under the skin, forming small lumps, faintly sensitive to the touch. Bullets or blades of weapons are supposed to be drawn to one of these magic lumps, from which they glance harmlessly off. There is some difference of opinion as to the proper number of needles to be let into the body, but it is generally agreed that an odd number must be used.

It can hardly be healthy to have a number of rusty needles wandering round in the interior of the human anatomy, but nobody seems to worry about that. To my mind, gems under the skin, compared with wandering needles in the body, form quite a delightful sort of charm.

In the *Phongsawadan*, a Siamese history compiled in 1783, wherein fact and fiction are very skilfully mingled, is to be found the following curious story.

In the year 1684, when a Siamese Embassy to France was at Versailles, Louis XIV gave a display of military marksmanship in their honour. This consisted in drawing up five hundred French soldiers in two opposite ranks of two hundred and fifty each, and ordering them to fire their muskets at one another. So accurate was their aim that each bullet went into the barrel of the corresponding musket in the opposite rank, and nobody was hurt.

"What would the King of Siam say to that?" asked King Louis. "Well," replied the chief Siamese Ambassador, "the King of Siam does not really care much for that sort of marksmanship. He relies more on soldiers who are able, by magic charms, to render themselves invulnerable. He even has a few who can make themselves invisible, and think nothing of penetrating into the ranks of a hostile army, cutting off the General's head, and bringing it back to His Majesty."

The King of France was incredulous, thinking that the Ambassador might possibly be exaggerating. He therefore enquired whether any of the invulnerable type of soldiers had come with the Embassy. The Ambassador explained that he had only some rather second-rate specimens with him, but promised to see what he could do. He would, he said, have a charm prepared for the next day, and would then be glad to let the French soldiers shoot at his men.

"But," objected King Louis, "it will cause ill-feeling on the part of your King if I have his soldiers shot." "Do not worry about that," replied the Ambassador, "leave it all to me."

The next day a magician who had accompanied the Siamese Embassy, together with sixteen soldiers, all carefully treated with anti-bullet magic, were placed on a raised platform. The magician was dressed all in white, while the sixteen soldiers wore red. At a given signal, five hundred French soldiers tried to discharge their muskets at the Siamese, but in every case the weapons missed fire. The French soldiers, terrified, flung down their arms. "Do not fear," cried the magician, "try again; this time the muskets will go off."

So they tried again, and sure enough all the muskets did go off, but not one single bullet reached the Siamese soldiers. The bullets all fell harmlessly to earth, some close to the muzzle of the weapon, some half-way to the platform on which the Siamese were seated, some close to the platform, but, anyhow, they all fell short.

King Louis was greatly impressed by this display of Siamese magic, saying, as well he might, that he had never seen anything to equal it. From that time onwards, he always believed whatever the Ambassador told him, and treated him with marked favour.

Siam is full of spirits, good and evil, but there are far more in the north than in the south. The Malays, themselves very well provided with ghosts and demons, for the most part only know of the Laos of northern Siam as a race of people who keep evil spirits in bamboo bottles to let loose on those who annoy them.

The average Lao would be the last person to deny that this is very often true, for a large number of people are generally supposed to harbour evil spirits and send them out to injure others, though I do not think they usually keep them in bamboo bottles. I have seen quite a number of people who were said to be under demonic influence, and they certainly behaved in a very queer way, though probably King James I would have seen nothing very unusual about them. The most important part of the treatment given to such cases used always to be to flog the spirit, or in other words to flog the person whom it was inhabiting, until it confessed who had sent it. The voice of the spirit was always quite unlike the normal voice of the victim, and it often said things which the latter could hardly have been expected to know.

This cure by beating is not encouraged by the Siamese authorities, but doubtless it is still practiced in country places.

When the spirit had been forced to reveal the name of its master or mistress, he or she was of course known to be a witch, and in former times was often killed, or at least driven forth to live in the jungle. I have seen several witch settlements in various places. A curious thing is that the inhabitants of such settlements are often by no means certain that they are not really witches. One old lady once told me that she was afraid she must be a witch, and that she did not want to be one at all, but could not help it.

Many English and American children, on first reading in the Bible about Jesus casting out devils, ask for an explanation, and are then told that being "possessed of a devil" was the same as being insane. This is quite a mistake. Some lunatics are possessed of devils, just as some fevers are caused by poison; but poisoning and fever are not synonymous terms. The biblical descriptions of demonic possession refer to a condition which is perfectly familiar to everyone in northern Siam. I have myself heard the voice of a devil begging for mercy from an exorcist, just as the Gadarene devils besought Jesus that he would not "command them to go out into the deep".

One of our servants was said to be a warlock and his mother a witch. Together, we were told, they had eaten out the livers of several people. I asked him about it, but he maintained that he had never eaten anybody's liver. We refused to dismiss him, though he was never popular with his fellow servants. I never saw him eat anybody's liver, but he once nearly bit off a syce's ear. The two lads were reputed to be good boxers, and one day after tennis some of us offered the pair of them a prize for an exhibition bout. They had not been at it for long when the wizard seized the syce's ear in his teeth, and refused to let go. I grabbed the wizard and another man the syce, and we pulled them apart with a loud snap. They bore no malice to one another after this, and the wizard personally rubbed ointment on to the syce's ear every day for a week.

A peculiar sort of spirit which sometimes takes possession of people is the *Phi Buay*. The victims of this sort of spirit remain perfectly normal in every respect but one—they absolutely refuse to wear any clothes. This condition is rare, and when it occurs in a town-dweller the person affected is found to be so inconvenient that his or her relatives usually arrange for a transfer to some country village.

I once met a young fellow walking along a country road, carrying a gun, and entirely naked. He seemed to be quite sane, and I exchanged a few civil words with him. Afterwards my servants told me that he was *Phi Buay* and that he was a very smart and well educated young man, who had been sent to live in the country by his relatives at Phrae, as the neighbours objected to the eccentricity of his garb— or lack thereof.

Some people I once met had a grown-up daughter who was possessed by the same sort of spirit. They were obliged to keep her in her room all day, and took her out for air and exercise in their back garden after dark. Some of the naughty boys of the village used to infuriate them by hiding behind bushes and lighting matches when she passed by. In these days of electric flashlights, young ladies afflicted by this distressing form of possession must be even more difficult to deal with.

The late Sir Hugh Clifford wrote some interesting stories about people suffering from that curious complaint called by the Malays *Latah*. *Latah* is not very common in Siam, but it exists, being known by the names of *Ba Chi* or *Ba Khi Krang*. People who are *Ba Chi*, if suddenly startled, become extremely liable to the power of suggestion, and will imitate the words or actions of those near them. An old woman I once knew, who had this complaint, was one day passing a police station, on the lawn of which a dozen policemen were being drilled by a sergeant. Just as the old dame came along, the sergeant gave a word of command in that singularly rousing tone of voice affected by sergeants all the world over. The old lady gave a jump, dropped her market basket, and started to copy all the movements of the policemen, quick march, right about turn and all the rest of it. The men laughed so much that the drilling had to be stopped until she had recovered and was able to go on her way. She was fearfully angry about it, and roundly abused the sergeant for having such a penetrating voice.

Lao people do not only keep *evil* spirits. Almost all of them keep good spirits in their houses, or spirits, at any rate, which do not bite the hand that feeds them—for spirits, of course, have to be fed, just like any other domestic animals. Families moving to a new house often go to some trouble and expense to induce a suitable spirit or two to come and live there and look after them, and almost every house has a neat little shrine in which offerings for the spirits are placed.

Different spirits have different characters. Some of them are more or less lax in their moral principles, but most of them tend to be dreadfully narrow and puritanical. Once when my wife and I were staying in a small village, an old couple living near by came to us in a very perturbed state of mind and complained that our cook had committed a horrible outrage in their house. We were greatly concerned, but on closer enquiry it was revealed that all our cook had done was to stroke the hand of their daughter. We said that we were very sorry our servant had annoyed them, but suggested that, after all, the young lady's reputation would perhaps not suffer serious damage owing to her hand having been stroked. "But, my dear Sir and Madam," said the old father, "you do not understand. We ourselves do not worry much over matters like this, if only your cook will make love to our daughter outside, and not in our house. We have a spirit living in the roof which is extremely strict in its morals, and which is rendered furious if it observes even the slightest familiarity between unmarried persons. After what it has seen today it will, in its rage, bring down all sorts of evils and calamities upon us."

So we had to pay several ticals to provide exceptionally spicy offerings for the propitiation of their spiritual Mrs. Grundy.

The cook was made to contribute too, and was very annoyed about it, evidently thinking that he had not had his money's worth.

The mother of one of our servants used to be possessed at times by a rather peculiar spirit called a *Phi Pokalong*. Possession by this species of spirit is not a thing to be avoided, as various benefits accrue to the person possessed. The old lady was able to tell when the spirit was about to take possession, and would hurriedly put on a pair of trousers, because that particular sort of spirit dislikes women, and will only communicate either with a man, or else with a woman who has diddled it into mistaking her for a man by the simple expedient of putting on trousers. Though so easily deceived in regard to a person's sex, the *Phi Pokalong* was exceedingly sharp in other ways, for it was able to tell where stolen property had been concealed, and even to indicate the thief: it certainly made one or two remarkably good shots, and was the means of recovering quite a lot of stolen property. The owners made handsome presents to the old lady, and I rather wondered whether she did not know more about the thieves than the spirit did. As a general rule, this spirit was very guarded in its replies about stolen property, and when describing the thieves adopted a style of super-Delphic ambiguity.

There are other occult ways of finding out thieves besides consulting a *Phi Pokalong*, which is rather a rare sort of spirit, and not always at hand when required. When we were at Singora, burglars broke into our house and stole some of my wife's jewellery. Our Siamese landlord assured us that if any of our servants were implicated he would spot the culprits. He accordingly prepared a number of small cakes, which, after suitable incantations, were placed for a night on the grave of a man who had committed suicide. Next day, all our servants were assembled, prayers were said, and each man was given a cake and told to eat it. They all swallowed their cakes with ease except one man, who was quite unable to do so; he turned purple in the face, broke out into a profuse sweat, and finally bolted from the room and spat out the cake in the garden. "Aha!" said our old landlord; "there's your man!"

Of course the landlord was right; but the worst of these occult arts is that modern courts do not recognize them. I could hardly go to the Siamese court to charge a man with burglary, and on being asked to produce my evidence, reply:

"I told him to eat a cake, but he spat it out in the garden." According to the rules of the game, the culprit would have died on the spot had he swallowed the cake. A few weeks later he *did* die, and our landlord always maintained that a crumb or two of the cake had slipped down his throat. Had he managed to avoid swallowing even a single crumb, he would have had a severe illness, merely by reason of his having had the cake in his mouth.

In northern Siam there are two sorts of spirits called *Phi Mot* and *Phi Meng*. Both these spirits are of Burmese origin, and the people who invoke them are probably—though they themselves do not know it—descendants of Burmese or Mon settlers who came to Chiengmai when it was a Burmese dependency (A.D. 1556 to A.D. 1775, with intervals). The spirits are called down by performing for them dances similar to the *Nat* dances of Burma. Only women take part in the dancing; some of the dancers are quite old, and often work themselves into a sort of hypnotic state, in which they act as mediums and profess to speak with the voices of departed friends; other performers are young women, and on the only occasion on which I witnessed one of these dances it rather seemed to me that some of them were paying a good deal more attention to a few lively young fellows among the audience than to the spirits. Although only women are permitted to take part in the spirit dancing, the *Phi Mot* and the *Phi Meng*, like the *Phi Pokalong*, appear not to be too fond of the fair sex, for sometimes the dancers can only induce them to manifest themselves by assuming male garb. They do not go so far as the old lady who wore trousers to bamboozle the *Phi Pokalong*, but merely put on a man's sarong over their skirts and tie coloured cloths round their heads—another link with Burma. This is quite enough to deceive a *Phi Mot* or a *Phi Meng*, which are altogether duller spirits than the *Phi Pokalong*, for they never discover stolen goods. On the other hand they can, I believe, often cure various kinds of sickness, and some of the dances are given in gratitude for such cures.

There are no werewolves in Siam, but there are were-tigers, which are much worse. In the Malay Peninsula were-tigers are comparatively common. I knew a young Malay at Patani whose father once put up an unknown traveller at their house. Suspecting that there was something uncanny about the visitor, my friend's father ordered him on no account to let him out of his sight. During the night the wayfarer crept out of the house; my friend crept after him and saw him hide behind a bush and let out a yellow and black striped tail! An alarm was given, whereupon the tail suddenly went back with a loud snap; but they took no more risks, and drove forth the *Rimau Jadi-jadian,* as the Malays call such folk.

In northern Siam, weretigers are called Süa-Yen. I have only met one of them, and he was not an indigenous specimen, but an Indian of eccentric habits named Ram Das. His eccentricity first showed itself by his posing as a Buddhist priest. Later on he took to chaffing small children and offering them cakes and sweets. I do not believe that he meant harm of any sort, but unfortunately for him two children disappeared from their homes at about that time, and somehow or other a rumour got about that Ram Das was a were-tiger, and that he had stolen the two children and eaten them. Next time he spoke to a child he was chased by an angry crowd, and narrowly escaped serious injury. I had him examined, and he was found to be insane, so I arranged for him to be sent over to the Mental Hospital at Rangoon. He was certainly an extraordinary looking person. When I saw him he had apparently not had a wash for years, and he certainly smelt very much like a tiger, only worse.

In England, if a man goes about dressed as a woman he is arrested, and it seems to be assumed that for a man to have a liking for female dress is a sign of some sort of moral perversion. In certain regulations annexed to the Indian Penal Code a similar assumption is made. In Siam, especially in the north, there are a certain number of men who habitually wear female clothing and grow their hair long. It does not seem to be thought that there is anything morally wrong about this, and so far as I have been able to make out, these *Pu-Mias* (men-women), as they are called, really possess, as a rule, no moral eccentricities. Physically also, I am told, there is nothing unusual about them. They prefer to dress as women, and that is all there is to say about it.

There used to be a young fellow of good family living near us at Lampang who sometimes dressed as a man and sometimes as a woman, and it was generally believed that during the first half of each month he actually was a male, and during the latter half of the month became a female. I often exchanged greetings with him (or her) and found her (or him) very pleasant and polite, but I never became sufficiently familiar to justify making personal enquiries as to his (or her) sex. To my eyes he appeared to be a young man of very attractive appearance, though a trifle girlish looking. He did not wear his hair long, but when sporting feminine costume was very fond of decorating his head with flowers.

Another *Pu-Mia* I used to know was quite different, being a great hulking fellow of exceptionally masculine appearance. He always dressed as a woman, wore his hair long, and affected the most ridiculous, simpering manners.

I read some time ago of an English *Pu-Mia* being chased by an angry crowd across Hampstead Heath, hauled up before a magistrate, severely lectured on the depravity of his conduct, and heavily fined. Here, thought I, is one of the things they manage better in Siam. Why bother about *Pu-Mias?* So far as I can see, they do no harm, and in Siam, where nobody worries about them or interferes with them, there is certainly very little of the sort of thing which their existence, on the English theory, might be taken to indicate.

Female *Pu-Mias,* who dress and behave as men, are not so common as the male kind. I have only met one of them. She lived at Lampang, and was a dependant of the hereditary Prince of that province. She invariably wore male costume, and did all sorts of heavy work in the Prince's palace, utterly despising every sort of feminine accomplishment. Like "Colonel" Barker, whose case attracted so much attention in England after the first World War, this *Pu-Mia* decided to marry, and asked the Prince for the hand of one of his female servants. The pair were duly wedded, and the "husband" worked hard to support his wife, and was said to be very jealous of any attentions which were paid to her. Finally she out-Barkered Colonel Barker by becoming the proud "father" of a fine baby boy.

To revert to spirits. Though I have had a great deal to do with them, am very skilful at exorcising them, and once shook hands with one of them, I have only ever seen one spirit—and that was the ghost of a little black dog.

When M. and I first came out to Siam we used, in the hope of thwarting the ubiquitous burglar, to make our servants take turns to sleep in the lower verandah of our house. Before long, they started to grumble about a little black dog which came at night to worry and frighten them. They scorned the idea that it might be a real dog which had somehow got in. In the end they gave up sleeping there, but the story always persisted that there was the ghost of a little black dog in the house. Later on C., who was living with me in the same house, several times asserted that he had seen a black dog run across his bedroom, and when he called his servant to chase it out, there was nothing there, though the door of his room had remained closed. A year later, L. repeatedly saw a black dog in the same room.

Some years after this, Judge H. and I were seated at the dining-table in the same house. H. was telling me an amusing story when he suddenly stopped short. I saw that he was looking fixedly at a particular spot in the verandah, and turning my gaze in the same direction, I saw a little black dog standing there up against one of the white stucco pillars. It vanished almost immediately. The light was good, and the little dog was quite clear and distinct. It was a dog of the pariah type, with stiff ears, though below the average size.

Of course everybody laughed at H. and me, and said that we had simply seen a pariah dog, which had then run away. But it was not a real dog, all the same, and it did not run away; it vanished.

In northern Siam there are as many kinds of mediums, psychometrists, astrologers and other professors of the occult sciences as there are in England or America. Both in the East and the West I have tried to test the powers of some of these people, but have not obtained any very interesting results in either hemisphere, though I still maintain an open mind on the subject. The difficulty in regard to these matters is that people who do not want to believe will believe nothing, while those who do want to believe will believe anything.

When we were living at Lampang, tremendous excitement was caused by the alleged manifestations of the spirit of a young man who had died some time previously. He had been engaged to a girl, and after his death he first made his spiritual presence known by an unpleasant habit of spitting on the young lady's shoulders. She would now and then utter a yell, and would then be found to have some human saliva on one of her shoulders. Apparently it never occurred to anyone to suggest that it might have come from her own mouth. She lived in a small house with her mother and a cousin; the latter was a lad of sixteen, and was a British subject, being the son of a deceased Burman. When the spitting performance had been going on for about a week, the young cousin fell ill, and a rumour was spread that the spirit of the deceased *fiancé* was haunting the house and had produced the boy's sickness. The spirit then began to show its presence by the miraculous production of numerous *apports*, such articles as boxes of matches, betel-nuts, small fruits, etc., appearing from nowhere. Crowds flocked to the house each evening, and a special spirit expert was engaged, who held seances of a kind there.

My wife and I went along one evening to see the performance, and were speedily rewarded by the appearance of a box of matches, which occasioned a gasp of mingled fear and admiration from the audience. I will not bore my readers by describing the architecture of a Lao house; suffice it to say that I at once saw that the *apports* could quite easily be produced by anyone standing in the inner room, the door of which was kept closed. I asked leave to go inside, which was granted, and I then proceeded to produce in the midst of the astonished company outside some nice little *apports* which I had brought with me, namely two small chrysanthemums, a walnut and a safety pin. I had supposed that the appearance of these small articles immediately after my entry into the inner room would make the nature of the deception evident to all present. Far from it! Instead of arousing any suspicion of fraud, my *apports* were acclaimed as final proof of the power of the spirit. We left it at that, bade a polite farewell, and went home.

Late that same night, a Burmese relative of the sick lad came and told me that in his opinion there was something suspicious about the attack of sickness. "Wait and see," he said, "the boy will die, and everyone will say that his death was caused by the ghost. He has plenty of property, and some at least of it will go to his aunt and cousin." A horrible fear came over me that I had perhaps been conniving, almost in a jocular way, at the commission of a murder. The Siamese High Commissioner from Chiengmai was at that time in Lampang. I sought him out and told him of my suspicions. He acted at once. A very strong hint was sent to the old lady that she would be wise to have no more production of *apports* in her house, and to remove her nephew to the hospital. The hint was taken. The spirit ceased its manifestations and was never heard of again, and the sick lad was sent to the hospital and got well.

Far be it from me to suggest that all *apports,* whether in the East or in the West, are fraudulent. Nevertheless, the following point is worth considering. The object of producing *apports* seems to be to prove the presence of a super-normal agency, yet the articles produced are usually such as can be obtained round the corner for a few cents. Let a spirit take the triple tiara from the Pope's head, or remove the regalia from the Tower of London, and plank them down on the dining-table of the President of the United States, and the hardiest scoffers and sceptics will be silenced forever.

About the most convincing *apports* I ever heard of or met with were my own chrysanthemums, regarding which a valid claim might have been made that they were flowers of a type quite unknown to the medium, and which she had no pro-bable means of procuring. In fact, had I not just produced them out of my own pocket, I almost think that their appearance might have convinced me of the genuineness of the manifestations.

Sometimes it is difficult to decide whether one is dealing with a natural or a supernatural creature. For instance, take the water elephant. I have never been able to find out whether this is supposed to be a living animal—albeit possessing uncanny powers—or a jungle spirit. One cannot be certain whether the creature is purely imaginary, or whether there really exists some kind of water-rat or mole bearing a super-ficial resemblance to an elephant.

This water elephant, or *chang nam,* is said to be found in distant jungle streams of northern Siam. It is a tiny beast about as big as a rat, but is formed exactly like an elephant, trunk, tusks and all. I never met anyone who claimed to have actually seen one, but it would be unreasonable to expect to do so, for the sight even of the animal's shadow is followed by the speedy death of the person seeing it. Moreover, if a man leaves a footprint in the sand or mud, a water elephant may come along and stab the impression with its tiny tusk; result, death to the owner of the footprint. The same result comes about if a water elephant stabs a man's reflection in the water.

In Burma also there are said to be some water elephants; they are there called *ye thin,* and I am told that stuffed specimens have occasionally been shown in Rangoon; but Europeans who have seen them say that these are made of frogs' skins stitched together, with little imitation ivory tusks attached.

Let us leave the mountain streams for the sea. The Gulf of Siam produces a good number of pearls. There is nothing strange about this, but it seems to us rather queer that some of the larger pearls should breed and bring forth young ones. Such, at least, is the generally accepted belief. People do not talk about pearls breeding as a strange or miraculous event. A man will say to you, quite casually: "These two little pearls were produced this year by a mother pearl I own. Last year it gave birth to three, but none of them are of much value. My neighbour has a better mother pearl, which produces fairly valuable babies." It is just as commonplace as saying that the cat has had kittens, and if one expresses incredulity, one is looked upon much as one would be for doubting the possibility of kittens being produced by a cat. There is no fraud involved, for the pearls bred in captivity, so to speak, rarely have any value; though, I may add, by careful feeding and nourishing they can be made to grow a bit.

I have seen a "mother pearl" which was said to be pregnant. It had a small lump on one side, which I was assured would in due time have a separate existence as a baby pearl.

Among the Malays, breeding pearls are widely believed in, and from time to time correspondence on this subject has been published in some of the Singapore newspapers. The scientific view, of course, is that a pearl is merely an inert mineral substance deposited by an oyster, possessing no life itself and being quite incapable of reproducing its kind. On the other hand, some Europeans have expressed a belief in the possible existence of breeding pearls.

At first, one is greatly impressed by the general acceptance of breeding pearls as mere ordinary, commonplace things; but then, if it comes to that, all sorts of things which we

Westerners regard as strange or uncanny are accepted in the East as ordinary and commonplace.

A friend of mine suggested that the belief in breeding pearls may have arisen from people miscounting their pearls. I do not think this is so, for mother pearls are often put away all alone in special boxes, wrapped in cotton wool with a little milk dropped on it, and left there to produce their young.

As for myself, when I am in the society of pearl breeders I *almost* believe in it, but not quite. This may be because an experiment which I made produced no result. I put a guaranteed mother pearl away in a sealed box for two years, complete with all the necessary accompaniments as laid down by the best authorities, but when I opened the box not even a single baby pearl had appeared to reward me for my long wait. Perhaps I lacked faith.

IX

Quelling the Ghosts

From the previous chapter, my readers will have seen that there is a very plentiful supply of spirits and ghosts in northern Siam, and that they intrude at every turn into the lives of the people, worrying them in a thousand ways.

It may be asked whether nothing can be done to remedy this regrettable state of affairs. Well, sometimes it is possible to quell or exorcise troublesome ghosts. I myself have had a little experience in this art. I will relate a few instances.

When my wife and I bought the land on which we are still living, we knew there was a ghost there, but this did not disturb us much, as every site has a ghost or two. Our ghost was the spirit of a man who many years before had been accidentally drowned by falling down a well. In Siam, spirits of persons who die by accident or violence are supposed to be of a vengeful and malicious nature, and we soon found that our ghost was no exception.

A few months after we had settled in, one of our gardeners was taken ill. He had fever, pains in his stomach, and other disturbing symptons. Medical treatment had no effect, so his wife, suspecting that the gentleman who had been drowned in the well was the source of the trouble, went along to consult our local medium. This medium is an elderly lady living nearby, who, for a suitable fee, is always ready to go into a trance. When she is entranced, a "control," referred to as "the Prince," takes possession of her, and she then warbles in a rather squeaky voice a series of improvised verses, which may be designed to meet any case; lost property to be recovered, matrimonial disputes to be settled, evil spirits to be propitiated. When our gardener's wife sought her aid, the medium went into her usual trance, and the "Prince", singing through her mouth, said: "I have beside me here the spirit of Ai Pan, the man who was drowned in the well, and he says he is very angry with your husband."

"What has my husband done?" asked the gardener's wife, trembling all over.

"What has he done!" sang the "Prince": "The other day he was working in Mr. Wood's garden. He saw a pariah dog. He threw a brick at it. He missed it. But that brick went bang through the middle of Ai Pan's stomach when he was taking his evening stroll, and if there is one thing more than another which Ai Pan dislikes, it is having bricks thrown through his stomach. Unless your husband propitiates Ai Pan with some generous offerings, you may as well order his coffin."

So the gardener's wife came weeping to us, and we of course provided a suitable meal of rice, pork and fruit for Ai Pan's spirit, together with a few candles to burn in his honour and some joss-sticks to tickle his sense of smell. When this had been done, the gardener recovered at once; but he was very careful not to throw any more bricks about.

But there was an even more dangerous ghost in the neighbourhood than that of Ai Pan. This spirit inhabited the garden of our neighbour, an Englishman named Henderson. It was the spirit of a woman who many years before had hanged herself on a branch of a mango tree. Henderson had a young fellow of about eighteen working for him, the son of a very respectable old man of our village. One day this lad fell ill, and his father, following the example of our gardener's wife, sought the aid of the medium. The "Prince", speaking through the medium's mouth, told the old man that his son had grievously offended I Kam, the lady of the mango tree, by slashing the bark of her tree with a knife.

"What must I do?" asked the old father.

"Try some very superior offerings," replied the "Prince",

"but judging by the way I Kam talked to me, and the ugly face she made, I warn you that it may be no use. I think she intends to have your son's life."

And so she did. The poor lad died a few days later.

So Henderson and I put our heads together. Here were our servants being made ill, and even killed, by vengeful spirits, and we thought it was time to seek a permanent remedy. In a neighbouring village lived a highly skilled sorcerer, even more competent than our local medium to grapple with troublesome ghosts. We sought him out and laid our case before him. He was very sympathetic, and after carefully considering the matter, told us that for a sum of twenty-four ticals (£2) he would prepare a raft, on which he would induce the malicious ghosts to embark, and would then let them float away down to Bangkok. Needless to say we readily closed with this offer.

On the day appointed, the sorcerer duly made his appearance. He was carrying a neat little bamboo raft, about three feet long. On it was a tiny bamboo house with a roof of grass thatch. He carefully put the little raft into the river in front of Henderson's house, and then proceeded to stock it with some rice, some small slices of pork, a few bananas and flowers, and a number of joss-sticks. He had brought along three young fellows to assist him. One of them had a flute, the second a small drum, and the third a two-stringed fiddle made from a coconut-shell.

Quite a large crowd assembled to watch the proceedings, and when all was ready the sorcerer read out an incantation, explaining the advantages of the raft and its little house, while his three young assistants played lightly on their musical instruments. Then the sorcerer raised his hands in supplication, and singing in a loud voice, invited the spirits to embark on the raft. At this point, the three musicians raised a tremendous din. The flautist blew his flute till he was purple in the face, the violinist fiddled for all he was worth, and the drummer banged his drum till I thought the parchment would burst. Amidst all this din, the two vengeful ghosts embarked unseen—or so we were told—on the little raft, the sorcerer gave it a push and away it floated. The crowd dispersed, feeling, as we did, that a good job had been well accomplished.

Where did the raft and its occupants float to? We shall never know; but this much we do know—the two ghosts have never been heard of since that day.

* * *

Although in the case of the gentleman ghost which so greatly disliked having bricks thrown through his stomach, and the lady spirit which was so fussy about her mango tree, we engaged a professional sorcerer to assist us, I hope it will not be supposed that I am incapable of tackling ghosts single-handed, and without any extraneous assistance. I have quelled unaided several troublesome spirits. Two instances of this may perhaps be found interesting.

In the foreign cemetery at Chiengmai there is the grave of an Englishman who many years ago was murdered by robbers. Near his grave stands an evergreen tree.

When I took charge of the British Consulate at Chiengmai in that year I found that one of the duties of the Consul was to manage the cemetery. My predecessor warned me on no account to meddle with the tree near Robinson's grave. He had, he said, once engaged a man to lop some of the branches of that tree, but the result was unfortunate, as the intruder had fallen from the tree and broken his leg. This misfortune was generally attributed to the anger of Robinson's ghost.

A few years later, the tree was looking very untidy, so I ventured to disregard my predecessor's advice, and engaged a workman, at about three times the usual rate, to lop a few branches. Hardly had my man climbed the tree when he fell off again, breaking three ribs. So I gave it up as a bad job for the time being.

Many years later, the tree had grown so big, and was so much in the way, that I determined to get rid of it altogether. A young man of my acquaintance, named Tan, told me that his father was not at all afraid of spirits, and would undertake to fell the tree if I made it worth his while. I agreed to his terms, and the old man started in with his axe; but hardly had he dealt a couple of strokes against the tree when he felt faint, so went home and retired to bed. He soon developed rather alarming symptoms, fever, pains in the joints, and swellings all over his body; his face, in particular, was very swollen and inflamed. The native doctor failed to cure him, so I asked Dr. McCall of the American Presbyterian Mission to have a look at him. Dr. McCall was puzzled by the symptoms, which were new to him; he tried various treatments, but in vain. So the sick man's son, feeling sure that Robinson's spirit was the cause of all the trouble, sought out a spirit doctor. No use at all! The spirit doctor told him that Robinson's ghost was certainly responsible for his father's illness, but said that he (the doctor) was powerless to intervene, as the ghost was that of a foreigner, and therefore not open to the influence of such spells and incantations as he could devise. In despair, young Tan came to me for advice. Needless to say, he found me ready to help him.

"Listen," said I, "you must know that English people have a prejudice against magic and sorcery, and for this reason I have always concealed the fact that I am a great expert in that line. Do not breathe a word to anyone, but come along to the cemetery at midnight tonight. You must bring a spade, a little rose-tree and six candles. I will bring a box containing a magic talisman. Keep silent when in the cemetery, and leave everything to me."

When he had gone, I prepared my little box containing the magic talisman. The box was wrapped up in white paper tied with red tape, and sealed. The talisman was a lump of sugar. At first I thought of putting in a pebble, but this seemed rather like sharp practice, so I used a lump of sugar. I also prepared a bottle of magic medicine. This was composed of water, with a little alum to taste nasty, and a little washing blue to look pretty. As in more orthodox medical practice, spirit medicine must look nice and taste beastly.

At midnight we met in the cemetery. There was no moon, but a good deal of thunder and lightning about; just the weather to create a suitable atmosphere. Tan had duly brought the spade, the rose-tree and the six candles, and we walked in silence to Robinson's grave. Here I made Tan put a candle at each corner, and two in the middle. Then he dug a small hole at the foot of the grave, and put in the rose-tree. Before the earth was filled in, I held up my little box, rattling it to show that the magic talisman was really inside. Then I laid the bottle of magic medicine on the grave, repeating in sepulchral and awe-inspiring tones these words:

> The boy stood on the burning deck
> Whence all but he had fled;
> The flames that lit the battle-wreck
> Shone round him o'er the dead.

At this point, there was a loud clap of thunder, and poor Tan clung to me, trembling in every limb and with his teeth chattering. I calmed him down, and made him fill in the earth round the rose-tree, after which we left the cemetery— one of us, at least, with huge relief—and proceeded to the nearby house of Tan's father. There the old fellow lay, all swollen up, and his son related to him, in quivering tones, the frightful experience he had just been through. Then I put my hand on his head and solemnly assured him that everything would be all right; his son had given the spirit a rosebush to compensate for the damage done to the evergreen tree; I had pronounced an infallible incantation, had buried near the grave a magic amulet of great power, and had prepared a special bottle of magic medicine, which had been laid on Robinson's grave. Let him take a dose of this twice daily, and a perfect cure would result.

I was right. The very next morning the swellings had subsided, and three days later the patient was reaping his field, in perfect health. He is still living, hale and hearty, today.

A religious friend of mine, to whom I related what I had done, accused me of having bowed down in the house of Rimmon. Maybe I did, but Rimmon or no Rimmon, I am quite sure that I saved the old man's life; and I feel fairly certain that the lump of sugar did the trick; a pebble would have been fatal.

* * *

Once, on one of my numerous Consular journeys in northern Siam, my wife and I camped for the night in a small village not far from Chiengrai. In the evening the village Headman, an unsophisticated old rustic, came along to see us. I could see that he had something on his mind, and after a little polite conversation he told me what was troubling him.

"Sir," said he, "I am a most miserable man. There is an evil spirit living in my rice-bin. It makes horrible moaning noises at night, and has terrified my wife into a fever, and made my little son come out in pimples all over. I even saw it once. It looked frightful, with hair all over it, and eyes like fire. I have called in three sorcerers to deal with it, and paid them a lot of money, but all for nothing; the demon is still there. Last week the English Forest Officer was here, and I asked him to help me, but he said he could not. If you can do nothing for me, I shall have to leave my home and move to another village."

"Cheer up," said I, "maybe I can do something. Of course the Forest Officer could do nothing; he knows all about difficult matters connected with forestry, but it is unreasonable to expect the poor man to know everything. If you want a man who knows everything, you must look for a British Consul. Yet even among that highly gifted body of men, there are some who have not studied occult sciences. I have! My uncle was Chief Sorcerer and Court Magician to the late Queen Victoria—the lady whose head you have seen on silver rupees—and when he died he bequeathed me his book of magic spells. I have it here with me now (here I held up a volume of Shakespeare's plays) and here on page 253 I find the following: 'how to get rid of evil spirits from rice-bins!' Just exactly what we want! Leave it all to me. I will get everything ready. Come along after dark and I will tell you what to do."

The old Headman went home, much relieved. After dark he came back again, and asked me if I was ready. I assured him that all would certainly be well, and then showed him a box containing twenty-one cartridges.

"Now, then," I asked him, "how many cartridges do you see there, and what colour are they?"

"I see twenty-one cartridges," he replied, "twenty of them are red, and one is black."

"Quite so," said I, "one is black ! The red ones are for shooting birds, and the black one, specially prepared by me according to the directions in my late uncle's magic book, is for, shooting evil spirits. Now come with me, and show me your rice-bin."

So off we went, I taking my gun. When we reached his house, he showed me his rice-bin, a small building standing a few yards from his house. I then put the magic black cartridge into the gun, and in solemn tones repeated these lines:

> The walrus and the carpenter
> Were walking hand in hand,
> They wept like anything to see
> Such quantities of sand.

Then I let off my gun, filling the rice-bin with magic No. 8 shot. This done, I once more assured the old fellow that there would be no more haunting, and went back to my tent.

Early next morning we proceeded on our journey.

Three weeks later we were returning along the same road. When we reached the village where I had shot the ghost, the old Headman and his wife—now cured—and most of the villagers came out to meet us, and gave us a reception almost worthy of royal personages. They brought us rice, eggs, chickens, and other presents, and could not do enough to show their sense of gratitude. This was because the magic cartridge had been one hundred per cent successful. The demon had disappeared, and so far as I know—for I was there again a few years later—it never came back to worry them any more.

So, as you will agree, I am fully competent to quell troublesome ghosts without any expert assistance. Moreover, I am the only sorcerer in Siam who performs this service free of charge.

After reading all this, maybe some people may wonder whether I believe in ghosts or not. Well, perhaps I do, for I shook hands with one once. But that, as Kipling said, is another story.

X

The Clammy Hand

I mentioned that I had once shaken hands with a ghost. Did I really do so, or did I dream it? Anyhow, this is how it happened.

Travellers in northern Siam like to camp near a Buddhist temple. It is always clean there. The next best place is in the neighbourhood of a police station. So when, one afternoon in June 1905, on a trip from Nan to Phrae, I arrived at the little village of Ban Wark, and found there an open green lawn, with a pretty little temple on one side and a miniature police station on the other, I quickly gave orders to unload my elephants, and set up camp there for the night.

The officer in charge of the police station proved to be an old friend from Phrae, Lieutenant Sanit. He strolled across while I was having my tea, and I, by way of being polite, expressed my satisfaction at the near presence of him and his men, in case any thieves or robbers might happen to be lurking around.

"Do not worry about thieves," said Lieutenant Sanit, "we rounded up all the bad characters in this district a couple of years ago. There was one tough fellow called Ai Nark who would have been after you for certain. He never stole anything but guns, and I see that you have at least two with you. Any sort of firearms were an irresistible bait to him. But he is dead. We shot him!"

As a matter of fact, I had three weapons with me, a .303 rifle, a 12-bore shot-gun, and a small revolver. When the time came to turn in, I leant the rifle against one corner of the tent, laid the shot-gun, in its case, under my camp cot, and put the revolver under my pillow.

I had not been asleep for very long when I was roused by the sound of something falling. Turning on my flashlight, I saw that my rifle had fallen over from its place in the corner of the tent, and was being slowly drawn away, stock first, under the flap of the tent. I leapt from my cot and seized the barrel. There was a slight resistance for a moment on the part of someone outside the tent, but I recovered my rifle. While this was taking place, I yelled lustily for aid. All my servants, as well as several policemen, came running up. I told them what had happened, and we all went outside the tent to see whether there were any traces of an intruder. All we saw was a stray cow, and the general consensus of opinion was that the cow had knocked against my tent, causing the rifle to fall over, and that I, in my half-awake state, had imagined the rest.

I, however, had some faith in my own senses of sight and touch. Before settling down again, I put my rifle under my mattress; any attempt to remove it from there was certain to arouse me at once. Moreover, I got my cook, who for many years had been a professional boxer, to bring along his mat and sleep on the floor of the tent at my side.

I had been asleep, perhaps, for half an hour when I was awakened by a slight shaking of my cot, and at the same time seemed to hear a faint clicking sound from beneath me. I sprang from my bed, incidentally putting my foot on my cook's face. He jumped up, and together we looked under the bed. My gun-case, which had been shut with the usual sort of catch, but not locked with a key, had been unlatched; the lid was open, and the barrel of the gun had been moved, and was lying across the section of the case containing the stock.

Once again the police left their slumbers when they heard us talking. This time, they seemed to be more impressed than they had been over the rifle, and offered to put a man on guard outside the tent. So with my cook on the floor by my side, and a policeman a few yards away, I once more composed myself to sleep.

But not for long! Once more I was awakened, this time by a sound like something moving under my head. I gently inserted my hand underneath the pillow, and touched—not my revolver, but a hand; and such a hand! All the concentrated coldness and clamminess of every horrible, cold, clammy hand in the world seemed to be collected and focused in that nasty hand.

I made no attempt whatever to hold on to the clammy hand, the touch of which was disgusting beyond description. I dropped it—though hardly like a hot coal—and yelled at the top of my voice. Once again, all the camp was roused, but there was even less to be seen than on the former occasion. My revolver had been moved from under my pillow to the edge of the cot. That was all.

But it was enough for me. The time was now 4 a.m., So I swallowed a stiff whisky and water, got out a book, and settled down to spend the rest of the night in my camp chair.

In the morning, Lieutenant Sanit, who had not been sleeping in the police station, but at his own house some distance away, and had heard nothing of what had passed, kindly came to ask me what sort of a night I had had.

"Not too good," said I, "I rather fancy that there was a thief hanging about trying to get hold of my firearms."

"Impossible!" he answered; "nothing of that sort has happened for more than two years, in the time of Ai Nark. But he is dead. I shot him and buried him myself."

"And where did you bury him, may I ask?"

"Why, right here, on this very spot!"

"Do you mean to tell me that you let me put up my tent right on top of the corpse of a dead robber?"

"Well, Sir, you had had all the trouble of putting the tent up before I came to see you. And, anyhow, I felt sure that there could not possibly be any unpleasant smell or anything like that. You see, Ai Nark has been there for two years and must be quite dry by now. Thoroughly desiccated, no doubt."

Thai boxing.

Photo: Peter Buranvityayawut, Chiangmai

A village temple, Chiengmai.

A young Lao priest.
This young priest is a friend of the
author.

The bamboo house.

Sing Keo feeding his spirit.

The author with one of his daughters.

Mrs. W. A. R. Wood.

"What!" I cried, "you have the nerve to stand there and tell me that he is dry! You have the audacity to assert that he is desiccated! Let me tell you that you are quite wrong. He is not dry or desiccated at all. He is clammy, frightfully clammy!"

XI

Before My Time

The city of Chiengmai was founded in A.D. 1296, and was the capital of an independent kingdom called Lannathai from that year until A.D. 1558, when it was occupied by the famous King Bhureng Noung of Burma. The State of Lannathai then became a Burmese dependency and remained in that position, off and on, until the year 1774, when the Burmese were driven out by King Taksin of Siam. The city of Chiengmai was deserted in that year, but became the capital of a Siamese vassal principality in 1794. It remained, for purposes of internal administration, practically independent until 1870. In that year the ruling prince, Kawilorot, died at a very convenient moment, for his somewhat arbitrary actions had seriously alarmed the government of the United States for the safety of their missionaries in northern Siam, and the Siamese Government wisely decided that the continued increase of foreign residents in the north might become a source of trouble unless Bangkok assumed a more direct control over the administration.

The first Siamese resident Commissioner was sent up from Bangkok in 1874, and a Siamese court of law was established at the same time, though many Lao laws and customs were allowed to remain in force until a much later date. For instance, the buying and selling of slaves was winked at long after it had been prohibited in southern Siam. I myself bought a slave as late as 1905. The transaction was, strictly speaking, illegal, but as I at once set the slave free, it did not greatly trouble my conscience.

The old Chief of Chiengmai were called *Chao Chiwit,* or Lord of Life; this is what they actually were, for they had absolute power of life and death over their own subjects. The following story was told me as to the last occasion on which this ancient right was exercised.

In the year 1874, shortly after the arrival of the first Siamese resident Commissioner at Chiengmai, the reigning Chief, being displeased with one of his retainers, gave orders that the offender was to be executed at dawn the following morning. It had never, up to that time, occurred to anyone to question such an order, but on this occasion someone suggested to the wife of the culprit that the powerful "King of the South" had sent a Commissioner to Chiengmai, who might be able to help her in some way. She accordingly went in the evening to see the Commissioner about the matter, and he at once declared that he could not and would not assent to the decapitation of any man who had not been properly tried and convicted. The Chief of Chiengmai had retired to bed, and nobody dared to wake him, but the Commissioner sent an urgent message to the officer in charge of the prisoner, forbidding him, in the name of the King of Siam, to carry out the Chief's order until further notice. Torn between fear of the King and fear of the Chief; the officer obeyed the Commissioner.

In the morning the Chief got up and had his breakfast He then bethought himself of the culprit, and sending for the officer in charge, he asked him how the execution had passed off. He was astonished to learn that the intended victim was still alive. "How is this?" he asked. "Your Highness, the Siamese Commissioner told me that the King of Siam would not approve of my executing him." "Oh, he told you that, did he? And what else did he tell you?" "Nothing else, Your Highness." "Do you mean to say he forgot to tell you that you were going to get a hundred strokes on your bare back with a rattan ? " "No, Your Highness, he didn't mention that." "Well, then, I am telling you so now." Then, calling another officer, he said: "Take this fellow and let the executioners give him a hundred strokes with a rattan, as hard as ever they can lay on;

and after that, let them cut off the other fellow's head."

As the Chief commanded, so they did; but it was the last time. No man has, since then, been openly slain for any offence committed in northern Siam, without at least the semblance of a trial.

The office of Hereditary Chief of Chiengmai has never been formally abolished, but after the death of the old Chief, Kaeo Navarath, in the year 1938, no successor was appointed, and the office has been allowed to lapse.

Many old Lao laws were retained for a long time. One of the early English residents in Chiengmai, Mr. L. T. Leonowens, the son of Mrs. Anna Leonowens of film fame *(Anna and the King of Siam)* having been ill, was carried through the streets for an airing, seated in a sedan chair. He soon found himself summoned before a local court, and charged, under an old law, with lese-majesty, inasmuch as nobody but the King of Siam or the Chief of Chiengmai was permitted to use this method of progression.

The following dialogue then took place:

"Is it true that you were carried through the city seated in a sedan chair?"

"It is."

"Are you the King of Siam ?"

"I am not."

"Are you the Chief of Chiengmai?"

"I am not."

"Then you plead guilty! The punishment provided by law for this offence is that your head shall be struck from your shoulders with a sword. Do you agree to this?"

"No, I think it is too severe."

"In that case, you must pay a fine of ten ticals."

Mr. Leonowens paid up.

This is not so incongruous as it appears, for under old Siamese and Lao law there was a regular system whereby almost any punishment could be commuted for a fine, and the fine was fixed according to the rank of the offender. Had

Mr. Leonowens been a prince, he would have been fined an enormous sum; had he held a title of nobility, the fine would have been considerable; as he bore no title, he ranked as a commoner, and therefore was fined at the lowest rate.

The system of trial by ordeal is one which has been in use all over the world, and traces of it persisted in England until the beginning of the nineteenth century, when trial by combat was actually permitted—though not carried out—in the case of *Ashford* versus *Thornton*. The learned author of *Stephen's Commentaries on the Laws of England* remarks, in regard to trial by ordeal, on the impiety of expecting the Almighty to perform a miracle whenever called upon by a litigant to do so. I humbly venture to disagree. It seems to me that a belief in the efficacy of trial by ordeal is a natural result of a belief in a just and almighty God. A man who cannot obtain justice from his fellow men, if he believes in a Higher Power, instinctively appeals to Heaven to vindicate his righteous cause.

Hard experience has at last, after many ages, taught mankind that the Deity is not in any way concerned with justice, as understood by man. Even those who trusted to ordeals were in fact admitting this, for Providence, if just, would not require men to fight or suffer owing to the wrongdoing of others.

The Siamese Law of Ordeals was put into its final form by King Phrajai of Ayuthia in A.D. 1536, and there was a similar law in force among the Laos. I am not certain when trial by ordeal fell into disrepute in southern Siam, but in the north I have met with several old people who, in their youth, had undergone this form of trial. One old Burman told me that he had been through the ordeal by water, in support of a claim to three teak logs. He and his opponent were both dressed in white, and after long incantations had been chanted by the experts in charge of the proceedings, they were ordered to dive into the Me Yome River. Two bamboos had been fixed to the bed of the river, so as to help them to stay under. My old friend said: "I clung very hard to the bamboo. My feet went up over my head, but stilll I clung there, with my eyes and my mouth very tightly shut, till my head was bursting, and my heart was making sounds like a great big temple drum. Then I let go of the bamboo, and rose up to the surface of the water. As soon as my head appeared, I heard all my friends shouting, 'He has won! He has won!' and saw them leaping about for joy. Then they took me out of the water, put garlands of flowers round my neck, and gave me the three teak logs. The other man only came up a few seconds before me. He was very much ashamed, but I was very pleased and proud. However, the next time a man tried to cheat me over some teak logs, I said, 'Let him have them! No more diving for me!'"

From what I knew of my old friend, I should think it quite likely that the three teak logs were not really his, in spite of the result of the ordeal.

Another old man I knew had more than once had cases decided by the ordeal of lighted candles. This kind of ordeal was a good deal less drastic than those by water or fire. All that was necessary was to light two candles, of course with appropriate ceremonies. The man whose candle burned longer won the case. I understand that great care had to be taken to see that there was no sharp practice. For instance, it was possible to bribe the judges to provide one candle with a thicker wick than the other, or a small hole might be bored through the side of one of the candles, through which water was inserted, damping the wick, and thus causing the candle to go out before its proper time.

I sometimes wonder whether the supporters of King Maha Chakraphat of Siam nobbled one of the candles when, in A.D. 1548, he decided his claim to the throne by this form of ordeal. This King, then called Prince Thien Raja, was a priest in a monastery, and was the uncle of the late king, a lad named Keo Fa. Keo Fa bad been murdered by his mother's paramour, who had then usurped the throne. Most of the nobility resented this, and a certain Khun Phiren formed a conspiracy to bring Prince Thien Raja from his monastery and make him

King. The Prince was a very religious man, and was unwilling to mount the throne unless he was assured of divine approval, so Khun Phiren arranged for an ordeal by candles. This was carried out at dead of night in a temple. Two candles were lighted, one representing the usurper and the other Prince Thien Raja. The usurper's candle was mysteriously extinguished, when burning its brightest, and the Prince therefore agreed to join the conspirators. The usurper was killed, and the Prince became King of Siam, with the title of Maha Chakraphat.

Khun Phiren himself later became King of Siam, as a vassal of the King of Burma, whom he had treacherously assisted to invade Siam. From all we know of his character, it seems extremely probable that he faked the ordeal by candles, by injecting water into the wick of the usurper's candle, so that the accession of King Maha Chakraphat was due to a trick, of which, however, we may assume he was himself quite innocent. The poor man had a very troublesome reign, and must often have wished that his own candle had been nobbled, instead of the usurper's.

I was once asked by the Siamese wife of an Indian Mahomedan, who had been accused of immorality, to arrange for an ordeal whereby her chastity might be vindicated. I am not sure what form of ordeal would be the proper one in such a case—fire, perhaps, as being the symbol of purity—but I declined to intervene, and suggested a mere commonplace action for slander. From what 1 knew of the lady, I doubted whether any form of ordeal would have done her character much good.

There is a lot to be said in favour of trial by ordeal. It is quick, anyway. The chief objection is that the wrong man so often wins. But this objection may be made in regard to any form of trial in any court in the world.

The modern custom of agreeing to settle claims by merely swearing the parties is, in principle, a form of trial by ordeal. Theoretically, the man who is in the wrong ought to die, as the Siamese formula has it, "in three days or seven days". In fact, he doesn't die, but there are still a few incurable optimists in Siam and elsewhere who hope he will. Or, maybe, the certainty that one's opponent will be damned hereafter is sufficient compensation for losing one's case. Personally, such a belief would not comfort me at all. I regard the sort of fellow who tries to do me down as certain to be damned, anyhow, without any need for special oaths to speed him on his way to hell.

Siam and Burma were at war, off and on, for over three hundred years. These wars seem to us now like very ancient history, yet I have actually met one man who took part in the invasion of the then Burmese State of Kengtung which was carried out in the year 1852. This was a very aged Lao prince, who informed me, during World War I, that he had offered to go to France with the Siamese Expeditionary Force, which was despatched in 1917. "But they did not want me," said he, "because I am too old; and in truth this modern style of fighting is very different from the fighting we went in for when I accompanied the Siamese army to Kengtung in the year 1852. Now they seem to fight in ditches; then we fought in the open; I, being a prince, fought on elephant back. One day my elephant, with me on it, was standing on a little hill, which the army of the enemy surrounded on every side. First the big guns went Boom, Boom, Boom, all round me. Then the little guns went Pip-Pip-Pip-Pip all round me. But do you think they succeeded in hitting me? Not a bit of it! They never even hit me once, nor did they hit my elephant; and what is more, they could not as much as hit the hill !"

"Prince," said I, "confess the truth to me; you had a magic amulet on you, and that is how you managed to escape the bullets of a whole army." "You have guessed right," he replied, "I *did* wear an amulet." "And did your elephant have an amulet too ?" "Of course it did, tied round its neck." "But, Prince, you told me that the enemy could not even hit the hill. Do you mean me to understand that the hill had an amulet too?" "Well, I am over ninety, and perhaps my memory may have played me false. Now that I come to think of it, maybe the hill *did* get hit in one or two places."

The Siamese Expeditionary Force of 1917 was composed entirely of picked men, all of whom had had a technical training of one sort or another. I thought of them in France, piloting aircraft, and driving tanks, while my venerable friend related to me about his elephant and his amulets, and the year 1852 seemed very far away. The old man died many years ago, and the war in which he took part is a long forgotten episode of ancient history.

XII

Elephants

All mankind may be divided into two categories. Those who know, or who think they know, something about elephants, and those who do not.

In northern Siam we all look upon ourselves as elephant fanciers, but the fact is that even people who have spent their whole lives looking after elephants often do not know much about them, and make the most amazing mistakes concerning them.

It is, perhaps, natural that human beings, who grab things with their hands, should find it difficult to understand an animal which grabs things with its nose.

What a wonderful thing it is, an elephant's nose, or trunk! No other animal, save man and the monkey, possesses so useful an organ. But it cannot compare with the hand, all the same. For instance, it is a mistake to suppose, as many do, that an elephant can pick up very small objects, such as pins, with its trunk. It can just manage to pick up a smallish banana, but even to do this it has sometimes to curl the trunk sideways and *sweep* the banana or other small object up, rather than really seize it with the two sides of the end of the trunk, corresponding to our thumb and forefinger.

An elephant depends for its very life upon its trunk. Cut off a man's hands and he can still live. Injure an elephant's trunk so that it pains the animal to use it, and the poor creature will soon die of hunger and thirst. All its food is gathered and stuffed into its mouth with its trunk, and it is unable to drink in any other way than by filling its trunk with water and squirting the contents down its throat. Not really a very convenient method. I have seen a case in which an elephant's trunk was under treatment for an injury, and in which the owner tried to keep the animal alive by feeding it by hand and using a squirt to give it water. The feeding was successful, but the squirting difficult to manage, and I think the elephant died from lack of water. However, the method seems to admit of possible success.

Elephants are not nearly so strong and robust as most people think. In proportion to their size and weight they are not able to carry or drag as heavy a load as a horse, mule, camel or man. This is partly due to the fact that they are ill-shaped for carrying or dragging purposes. No howdah has yet been devised which fits an elephant's back at all cornfortably, and which does not tend to slither about in all directions, and in dragging logs, for instance, an elephant's centre of gravity is in the wrong place relative to the log, and it cannot therefore use its strength to the best advantage.

Elephants are rather delicate creatures. They are liable to all sorts of illnesses and diseases, and their condition has to be carefully watched when they are continuously employed on hard work. Moreover, they bear extreme heat very badly, and are often attacked by sunstroke or heat apoplexy. In their natural state they travel and feed mostly by night, and during the heat of the day they loiter about in some shady spot, smearing themselves with nice cool mud, or powdering themselves with dust. Compel them to work in hot sunshine for any long period of days, and their health is certain to suffer.

Elephant owners in northern Siam, especially the teak firms, give their elephants a complete holiday during the hot season of the year, about February to May, and have special rest-camps for them in distant glades of evergreen forest, where food is plentiful. Only by doing this can the elephants be kept working year after year.

When an elephant is attacked by sunstroke it shows great

signs of distress, trembling all over in a manner very painful to behold, and finally lying down. An elephant which has been cruelly overworked or fatigued sometimes shows similar symptoms, and in either case the animal is almost certain to die if left where it lies down. This seems to be partly due to a kind of weakness of spirit or fatalism in elephants; they cease to struggle, and literally "give up the ghost". If, however, the suffering animal can be induced to stagger to its feet, and is taken to a shady place, where it is fed and watered, it is very likely to recover, though it may be a long time before it can work again. To force a fainting elephant to its feet, and thus give it a chance of life, all sorts of brutality are employed, such as burning it with a red-hot iron, or throwing pepper into its eyes. If by the infliction of sudden agony it can be induced to rise, its life may be saved; otherwise—almost certain death.

There was formerly a tusker elephant named Pu Ban attached to the British Consular transport at Chiengmai. Though a very fine-looking animal, he was rather liable to sunstroke and fits of giddiness, and one year I had a huge straw hat made for him. He looked very raffish when wearing it, and was much jeered at by small boys in the villages through which he passed on the march; but the effect was very satisfactory.

Elephants need very little sleep, and usually take it from about one or two in the morning till just before daylight. They lie on their sides, and while sleeping they breathe very heavily and noisily. Sometimes, when elephants have been tethered not far from my tent, I have crept out quietly in the small hours of the morning, to peep at them as they lay asleep. To me, there is something very pathetic about sleeping elephants; they are so big and so noisy, and yet so gentle and so helpless, and ready to leap to their feet in alarm if disturbed by any passer-by, human or animal. Near villages they seldom get a good night's rest, for pariah dogs prowl around and disturb them; and once they are roused, they rarely go to sleep again.

The intelligence of elephants is of a peculiar kind, quite different, for instance, from that of dogs. Even the dullest elephant can be taught to do things which in any other species of animal would be thought very clever tricks, but there are some quite simple things they never seem to learn. For instance, any elephant can kneel down and get up when told to do so, or pick up any object on request, but few of them learn to go for any distance along a road with their fellows, as a horse or bullock can, without a man on their neck to guide and direct them. Moreover, like some more stupid creatures, they seldom have the sense to stay where there is good food, but will often wander, when turned loose, looking for food among rocks and sand, and neglecting a plentiful supply nearby.

Elephants possess some powers that seem almost uncanny. For instance, when travelling with a howdah on its back, an elephant will rarely run the howdah against an overhanging branch. Sometimes it will stop and wait if it thinks there is any danger of doing this, and if the mahout taps the branch with his goad, the elephant will pass underneath, perhaps with only half an inch to spare. Now to calculate the distance of the branch from its own back merely by listening to the sound of a tap is remarkable enough, but that the elephant should allow, in addition, for an extraneous object such as a howdah seems almost incredible. Yet I have seen this happen hundreds of times.

I am not sure that elephants really possess such wonderful memories as is generally supposed, nor am I certain that they treasure up, as the stories relate, feelings of gratitude or revenge, as the case may be. I have met with several instances of elephants killing or injuring men, either their own mahouts or strangers, but in every case the incident was, I believe, due to sudden anger or nervous irritation. Some elephants are naturally irritable and nervy, and some abnormally liable to go *musth*. Others are naturally fierce or savage, and always need to be carefully handled.

The cause of the condition known as *musth* in male elephants is very imperfectly understood. The principal outward symptom is the discharge of an oily secretion from a small hole near the animal's eye. It is almost certainly connected with the sexual functions, and a similar condition is met with in some species of deer during the rutting season. Nevertheless, male elephants breed freely at any time, not only when they are *musth*. Whatever the cause, the condition makes all elephants, even the tamest and mildest, more or less fierce and untrustworthy. A clever mahout can tell if an elephant is about to become *musth* some days before the discharge appears, and will take proper precautions to avoid danger.

Savage elephants are a constant source of danger, and it is marvellous how mahouts are found to ride such animals, considering that even in special cases the work is not very highly paid. I fancy some do it from a kind of bravado, and are inclined to swank because they are in charge of an elephant which has already killed a few men, and may any day kill another.

I once saw a man killed by an elephant, and once was enough. The elephant, a big tusker, was in a timber camp belonging to one of the teak firms, and was *musth* at the time. Its mahout went up to try to mount it, offering it a sort of cake to propitiate it. The elephant took the cake and ate it, and then suddenly seized hold of the man with its trunk, and laid him—not roughly—across its two tusks, with the trunk over him. I do not think it meant to hurt the man, and he himself kept his head and did not struggle or cry out; some of the less experienced bystanders, however, started shouting and yelling, and threw sticks, knives and axes at the elephant, hoping to make it drop their comrade. This infuriated the elephant, which again seized the man in its trunk, and this time drew his body two or three times on to its tusks, passing them through him. It was the most fearful sight I have ever seen. The elephant finally flung away the dead and shapeless body and went quietly down to a stream near by, where it calmly proceeded to wash its tusks.

A Siamese friend of mine saw a similar incident at Nakawn Srithammarat in the Peninsula. There was an old elephant there which had been taught to drink *samshu*—as though elephants had not got bad habits enough of their own, without teaching them ours as well. When passing a certain liquor shop, this elephant used to lift up its trunk, and the owner of the shop would give it a glass of *samshu*. One day a customer, who had had a drop too much, held out a glass of *samshu* to the elephant, but just as it was about to take it from him, he drew it back and drank it himself: The elephant immediately seized him, and before anyone could stop it, killed him in the manner described above, by pulling him up and down on its tusks.

Some elephants, which are not really savage, have a horrible habit of swinging their bodies and heads from side to side in order to shake off their mahouts. It is quite impossible to describe this performance, which is terrifying in the extreme to behold. Only very expert riders can stick on when an elephant *swais,* as it is called, and if thrown off, they fall to the earth with force enough seriously to injure or even to kill them. It is very difficult to cure an elephant of this bad habit, but a smart mahout can usually see a few seconds ahead when the performance is likely to begin, and will quell the elephant into good behaviour by sundry deft blows or thrusts in some tender spot.

A certain amount of brutality seems to be unavoidable in dealing with specially savage or intractable elephants, but an enormous majority of elephants can be managed much better by kindness. I have been in charge, at different times, of fifteen elephants, and only one of them required any great strictness of control—I am speaking of normal circumstances, not occasions of *musth* or other special emergencies. As a general rule, I never allowed my mahouts to be rough or brutal with the elephants. I was usually successful in getting very good mahouts; many of them worked under me for years, and between them and their elephants a real attachment often existed, quite touching to see.

To what age does an elephant attain? This is a very vexed question, but I may say at once that most experts are extremely doubtful about the truth of the tales told in India and elsewhere concerning centenarian or even duocentenarian elephants. So far as I can see, an elephant's age is very similar to that of a human being. When twelve years old or so, it will perform light work; from about twenty to forty-five, it will be at its fullest working strength; up to about sixty, it will still be capable of making itself useful, if not overtaxed; after the age of sixty, it will not be of much use; between the ages of seventy and eighty it may be expected to die.

Many elephants employed in teak forests—I do not refer to those belonging to responsible firms, but to those owned by certain forest contractors—are habitually overworked, and do not, therefore, attain to their normal age, but die at about fifty or so.

To a man who understands elephants, an old animal looks very different from a young one. Its muscles are shrunken, it has deep hollows on its head, its skin is cracked and its trunk is thickened and lacking in suppleness. Elephant copers sometimes doctor up old animals to look like young ones, and have been known to take in the unwary. A man I knew, who rather fancied himself as an expert, was once offered what he took to be a handsome young elephant. Being short-sighted, he failed to observe that it had been polished up with oil and varnish, and that the deeper cracks in its sides had been payed out with tow and plaster. He agreed to pay a good price, and went next day to the Siamese District Officer's Court to pay the money and have the transfer paper made out. But while the District Officer's clerk was writing out the transfer paper, the poor veteran elephant lay down outside and died of old age.

Some elephants have other bad habits besides shaking off their riders; for instance, biting one another. One of the British Consular elephants had a taste for biting off her friends' tails, and when travelling, fearful screeches and trumpetings in the jungle at night were usually taken as a sign that Me Ngorn was having a go at another elephant's tail. Hardly any elephant came within her orbit without having at least a few hairs pulled forth, and finally she managed to get in a real good snap, and bit another female elephant's tail clean off, some eight inches from her body. The poor victim bad to go about till the day of her death with a horrible little tail like a pig's.

Another Consular elephant developed a ghoulish habit of digging up and devouring human corpses. It came on quite unexpectedly. One morning she was found in a cemetery, near a dug-up grave, with pieces of half-eaten corpse all round her, and her body plastered over with putrid blood. It was a most loathsome business. It took hours to clean her up, and her mahout, who was a sensitive man, was ill for several days after it. To add to our troubles, the friends and relations of the corpse came along and said nasty things to us.

After that, we kept a sharp look-out on this ghoulish creature, and on one or two later occasions only managed, in the nick of time, to prevent her from repeating her exploit.

In every other respect this elephant was a most tractable and lovable animal.

I have spoken several times about elephants being loose in the jungle, and perhaps I ought to make it clear that no elephants in Siam, except the white elephants of the King, are as a rule kept in stables. When not working, they are hobbled on their forefeet and turned loose to feed themselves in some place where fodder is plentifuL When travelling, efforts are made to stop and camp only in places where elephant fodder is abundant, and the animals are turned loose at night, and caught again early the next morning. Sometimes they stray, and this causes great delay, for it is astonishing how much ground a hobbled elephant can cover in the course of a few hours.

When near a village, padi-field or plantation, the elephants have to be tied up to trees and fed with such things as coco-nut tree branches, banana trunks, jack-fruit twigs, and sometimes padi.

Not infrequently, elephants which have been let loose at an apparently safe distance from fields or plantations wander back and do damage to crops, which leads to the enforced settlement of more or less expensive claims. Often, too, the owner of a vegetable garden will lure an elephant on to eat or trample down a few cents worth of vegetables. This will form the ground for an enormous claim—but it can probably be settled pretty cheaply in the end.

The custom of turning elephants loose in the jungle renders it quite an easy matter to steal them, and in former times statistics of elephant thefts were an annual feature of Consular Trade Reports. Some comic papers, including *Punch,* again and again made jokes on this subject, apparently under the impression that an elephant is difficult to steal, whereas in fact this is far from being the case.

Elephant owners did not find the matter at all funny, and the poor elephants found it, if possible, even less amusing, for the thieves, in order to make them hasten, usually beat and maltreated them in a most brutal fashion.

Of late years, owing to the increased efficiency of the Siamese police, and partly also owing to the invention of a new method of permanent branding, elephant theft is no longer a common offence. It is as easy as ever to *steal* an elephant, but not so easy to get away with it, or to dispose of it in Siam or Burma without detection.

In the old days elephant thieves acted as follows: they would mark down an elephant which had been turned loose in the jungle, choosing, of course, a quiet and tractable beast, and would make friends with it by secretly giving it cakes or fruit. Their operations would be aided by the fact that many mahouts, though supposed to bring in and bathe their elephants each evening, often omit to do so for two or three days. Choosing a night just after an elephant had been bathed, and was therefore likely to be left alone for a day or two, the thieves would quietly go up to it, undo its hobbles, mount it, and drive it away as quickly as possible. Usually they took it to some distant Karen village among the mountains between Burma and Siam, and would keep it there for a year or more, until the brand marks had become faint—a process which can be artificially hastened—and would then take it to sell either in Burma or Siam.

To discourage pursuers, it was usual for elephant thieves to plant sharp bamboos, or even iron prongs, in the beds of any streams they crossed. The pursuers, if any, were usually walking barefoot, and a sharp bamboo or prong would so wound their feet as to prevent them from going on. I have seen a man with both his feet pierced clean through by elephant thieves' bamboos.

Sometimes the thieves made mistakes. The Forest Department at Chiengmai once let loose two female elephants very similar in appearance, but one of them quite tame and the other extremely savage. The thieves doubtless marked down the docile elephant as an easy prey, but in the darkness made an unfortunate mistake and tried to unhobble the fierce one. She was found in the morning, still hobbled, trampling slowly and methodically under foot a crushed and shapeless mass of flesh and bones which had once been an elephant thief.

A party of men in charge of some elephants, finding one animal missing, set forth post-haste on its tracks. A few days later they returned with the elephant, and reported to its owner that it had been stolen, but that they had brought it back. They explained that they had followed its tracks for two days, and had then suddenly come upon it, tethered to a tree in a small jungle clearing, whereupon they had untethered it and brought it home. "But how about the thieves?" asked their master, "did you see anything of them? " "No, we saw nobody at all." "But did you not see any sign or trace of them?" "Well, we *did* see a little tent not far from the elephant." "But was nobody in the tent? " "We do not know; we did not look; we just fired off all our guns through the tent. Nobody came out, so we untethered the elephant and came back home."

This story is very typical of the reluctance of country people in Siam to make unnecessary admissions, which may lead to awkward consequences.

An extraordinary thing about tusker elephants, even some fairly fierce ones, is that they seem to have no objection to their tusks being sawn off! It is not unknown for thieves to approach them in the night and quietly saw off their tusks, a good pair of which may be worth a very large sum. A man I once knew had an elephant loose near his camp; during the night it was heard to trumpet, but as this elephant was in the habit of trumpeting for no special reason, no notice was taken. In the morning, my friend found that the elephant's tusks had been sawn off. But the astounding part of the affair was that the thieves, greedy to get as much ivory as possible, had at first tried to saw too high up, and had penetrated that part of one of the tusks in which are found nerves and blood vessels; this had evidently caused the elephant to trumpet with pain, yet the foolish beast, even after that, had stood still while the thieves went on with their operations on a less sensitive part of his tusks. As the tusks of an elephant are an important natural means of self-defence, it indeed seems strange that some instinct does not prompt the animal to try to preserve them against amputation by thieves.

It is curious that some male elephants should have tusks and others none. Among other animals the characteristic features of the males are constant—I do not speak of individual exceptions—but tuskless elephants are quite common. In Siam they are called *Sidaw* and in Burma *Hlaing*. There are two kinds of Sidaw, those with short tushes, like some females, and those with no tusks or tushes at all. The son of a tusker may quite likely be a *Sidaw,* and vice versa.

Sidaw elephants are in no way lacking in virility; on the contrary, some experts say that they are particularly fond of the other sex. A *Sidaw* elephant belonging to the British Consulate at Chiengmai became in a few years the father of five calves, two of which were tuskers.

A *Sidaw* elephant is quite ready, when angered, to fight against a tusker, and sometimes wins, unequal though the contest may appear to be. I have heard of a *Sidaw* seizing the tusks of a rival with its trunk and breaking them off.

Elephants are slow walkers. Even when unloaded, they do not move as quickly as the average man. Loaded, they will not usually cover more than two miles an hour over hilly country. In really mountainous places their rate of progress is almost indescribably slow. On a slippery descent they are extremely nervous, and usually proceed by sitting down and tobogganing on their hind-quarters, always using their fore-feet as a brake.

As for running, an elephant can get up a great speed for a sudden dash or onrush, but it cannot maintain this for any great distance. An elephant could give a man a ten yard start over a forty-yard course, and beat him: but the man could give the elephant a twenty-five yard start and beat it over a two hundred-yard course.

An elephant cannot jump. Both the high and the long jump are beyond it. It can scramble over pretty high walls and mounds, but a trench four feet wide by six feet deep forms for it an absolutely insuperable obstacle.

A female elephant is pregnant for from eighteen to twenty-two months. The period of pregnancy is said to be longer in the case of a male than of a female calf, but I am not sure of this.

It is not easy to tell when an elephant is pregnant, and almost impossible to say, from the appearance of the animal, what is the approximate period of pregnancy remaining. I once called in a committee of alleged experts to examine a female elephant suspected of being pregnant; they all agreed that a calf was to be expected, but were emphatic in stating that it was not due for over a year. The baby elephant, however, confounded them all by appearing in the world only a week later; it was a particularly fine infant, too.

Every animal except the elephant creeps away by itself and wants to be alone when its young are born, resenting fiercely any intruder, whether of its own or some alien species. Not so the mother elephant. Her lady friends will gather round to help her in her labour, squirting water over her and covering her with mud, dust and other elephant cosmetics. When the baby is born, all the aunties, cousins and lady friends will help with its toilet, and will act as wet nurses if they are able. When it is bigger, its mother's friends will make a pet of it, and will often be much fussier about it than its own parent, trumpeting and running about if it happens to stray, or if it does anything which they consider dangerous or bad for it.

So far as I have seen, the paternal instinct is entirely absent in elephants. The father of an elephant calf looks upon his offspring in no other aspect than merely as an infernal nuisance.

I entirely agree with elephant papas on this point. Young elephants really are an infernal nuisance in every way. The worst of them is that they look small, simply because one compares them with grown-up elephants, whereas in fact they are big, clumsy creatures. Ladies say: "Oh, look at the darling wee pet!" But when the wee pet playfully barges into them and sends them sprawling, they do not find it quite such a darling.

Personally, I am very afraid of baby elephants, and never dare to go near one of them without arming myself with a long and stout cudgel.

As may be supposed, medical and surgical treatment of elephants is quite a big undertaking. Pills and potions are administered on a heroic scale, and the applications of salves and unguents often seems more like an agricultural than a medical undertaking. As for surgery, it is quite a tough job. Even to lance a biggish boil on an elephant requires the use of a large knife, and to put a few stitches into a wound is quite a fatiguing performance. The only time I ever did it, I used catgut out of a tennis racket.

On the other hand, sick or wounded elephants are often wonderfully tractable and docile, seeming to know that the nasty pill and the painful knife are for their good. Many an elephant will readily permit itself to be hobbled "fore and aft" for painful surgical or antiseptic treatment, knowing that it cannot refrain from instinctive kicking if its limbs are left unhampered.

A dead elephant is a pathetic sight—there is so much of it. I mean a dead tame elephant, for I never heard of anyone seeing the corpse of a wild elephant which had died a natural death. A tame elephant when dead is as inconvenient as it is distressing. If the animal has died from anthrax or some other contagious disease, it is dangerous to bury the corpse near a town or village, yet almost impossible to move it far. Cremation presents great difficulties. In one case, I had a dead elephant dissected by twelve professional butchers, and then removed in sections to be buried. One dead Consular elephant I successfully cremated. It happened to die in a narrow ravine in the jungle, and we piled thousands of logs and branches round and over the corpse, producing a blaze which must almost have equalled in magnificence the pyre of Sardanapalus. Never shall I forget the smell of burning flesh, pervading the air for miles around.

Everybody knows that Siam is the land of the White Elephant. In fact, however, not only the animal itself, but even the very name, is a Western invention. There never has been such a thing as a white elephant, and no Siamese ever speaks of such a creature. The animals which are venerated by old-fashioned Siamese, and some of which are kept in the royal palace as appurtenances of royalty, are in fact *albinos,* and are called by the Siamese *Chang Phüek,* which simply means " Albino Elephants". Albino buffaloes are very common, and they also are called *phüek*; the same word is used for human albinos. The idea of a "white" elephant probably originated from the old Siamese flag, but the animal shown thereon was, of course, merely an imaginary heraldic creature, like the unicorn.

It is not altogether clear on what grounds albino elephants are regarded with such high respect, nor when and how they became associated with royalty in Siam and Burma. The usual theory is that they are supposed to be reincarnations of former kings or princes. Strict Buddhists, however, reject this theory, which they say is of comparatively modern origin, and has merely been invented to explain an ancient custom, the true origin of which is obscured by the mists of time.

The first King of Siam definitely recorded to have owned a white elephant was Trailokanat of Ayuthia, who captured one in the year 1471.

These so-called white elephants are of a mottled pinkish colour, which often covers only part of their bodies, the rest being of normal tint. By far the best specimen I ever saw was Pawa, a young female elephant from Burma, which was shown in the Zoological Gardens in London in the year 1926, and died not long after in America. Pawa was pink all over, and was in every respect a most perfect and beautiful animal. In my humble opinion, it is doubtful whether such a perfect white elephant as Pawa ever existed before. It is quite certain that there are none now living which can equal her. It was a crime to take this unique elephant away from the tropics.

I say "humble opinion" because the points of a white elephant are, in Siam, an extremely tricky technical matter, only to be understood by a few experts. An elephant which you or I might hardly deem worthy to be classified as "white" at all may rank, in the eyes of an expert, well above another which to us appears infinitely superior in its degree of albinoism.

In the year 1926 a baby elephant of peculiar tint was brought forth by a female elephant belonging to the Borneo Company in one of the teak forests leased by that firm near Chiengmai. It was pronounced by experts to be a "white elephant", and as such, following immemorial custom, it had to be presented to the King of Siam. To comply with historical precedent, the official presentation had to be made in Bangkok by the hereditary Prince of Chiengmai. It so happened, however, that King Prachatipok and Queen Rambhai Bharni visited Chiengmai early in 1927, and a private presentation of the young elephant was made on the occasion of their visit by Mr. D. F. Macfie, manager of the Borneo Company.

I was present when this presentation took place. For some time before the King and Queen arrived, the young elephant was vigorously washed and polished, and by this means its peculiar reddish colour and light, almost bluish, bristles, were shown off to the best advantage. It was in a very frisky mood, and during the course of the preliminary proceedings knocked Mr. Macfie down, and pushed me and two other men into a ditch. We were all very nervous about its first meeting with the King and Queen, as it would never have done for the young elephant to behave roughly towards them, and men were standing all round prepared forcibly to quell the rampageous infant if it showed the slightest signs of being naughty. As it turned out, the behaviour of the little elephant was perfect; one might almost have supposed that it knew it was in the presence of royalty. The King offered it a piece of sugar-cane, whereupon it first raised its little trunk, as though in salutation, and then accepted the dainty in the quietest and politest fashion. After that, the Queen patted and fed the little elephant, and it never showed any sign of roughness during the whole time their majesties were there.

It is popularly supposed to be a good omen for a "white" elephant to be presented to a King during the first year of his reign, as was done in the case of the Borneo Company's elephant, and great jollifications were held at Chiengmai and later at Bangkok, whither the new mascot, with its mother, were sent by special train. It is sad to reflect that the good omen proved to be false. King Prachatipok, one of the noblest and most high-minded men who ever sat on the throne of Siam, was constrained by political complications to abdicate after a reign of only nine years, and died in England.

One of the white elephants of King Rama VI, who died in 1926, was a very savage creature. It several times smashed up rickshaws, carriages, and even motor-cars, in the streets of Bangkok. Its end was a tragic one. It escaped, and when pursued managed to jam itself between a pontoon and the river bank, where it was drowned.

Elephants, of course, can swim very well, and often have to do so across large rivers or streams. They look very curious when swimming, only part of their bodies appearing now and then above the surface of the water, with a slow, rolling motion, like porpoises. The trunk is kept all the time upright, with the end well above the water.

Elephants, "white" and black, march majestically up and down through the pages of Siamese history. King Maha Chakraphat, who reigned from 1549 to 1569, and who spent most of his reign fighting against Burma, captured and trained over three hundred elephants, more than had been owned by any of his predecessors. Among these were no less than seven white elephants, and King Maha Chakraphat therefore assumed the title of "Lord of the White Elephants". This irritated the King of Burma, who at once sent envoys to demand two of the elephants, alleging that a white elephant had been sent to Burma by a former King of Siam in the thirteenth century as a sign of vassalage. The King of Siam refused to comply, which brought on a very sanguinary war; Siam was invaded by an immense Burmese army, and in the end Ayuthia, then the capital, was captured, and the King of Siam reduced to a state of vassalage. Moreover, four of the seven white elephants were taken away to Burma.

When kings and princes took part in a war, they usually fought on elephant back. Queen Suriyothai, the wife of King Maha Chakraphat, was killed when leading an attack against the Burmese army in 1549, being pierced through by a spear and flung down from her elephant.

In 1592 King Naresuan, one of the great national heroes of Siam, engaged in personal combat with the Crown Prince of Burma, both combatants being mounted on elephants. The King's leather cap was cut through by the Burmese Prince, but on the second charge the Prince was thrown from his elephant and killed. The sword used by King Naresuan on this occasion, as well as his leather cap, used to form part of the regalia of Siam.

In 1622 the Cambodians captured over two hundred and fifty living elephants from the Siamese, besides killing a large number, and in some other wars thousands of elephants are said to have been employed.

At the present time, elephants are gradually dying out, and it would be difficult to collect them together by thousands, as in former times. The largest collection of tame elephants I have ever seen was in the year 1927, when the King and Queen of Siam visited Chiengmai. On that occasion, their majesties entered the city with a procession which included eighty-four elephants, among them the four Consular elephants belonging to King George V of England.

A great deal of time was spent in training the elephants for this procession, as it included several bands of various kinds, and many elephants tend to bolt when they hear unaccustomed noises. For a fortnight ahead the eighty-four elephants had to have drums beaten and trumpets blown close to their ears, and those which showed an obstinate dislike of these sounds were relegated to the tail end of the procession. We were all rather nervous when the King arrived, fearing that, even after their intensive musical training, some of the elephants might bolt and throw the whole cortege into confusion; but it all went off very well, and if the procession pleased the King and Queen as much as it did the loyal citizens of Chiengmai, they must have been feeling very happy.

To anyone accustomed to seeing elephants in more or less natural surroundings, the appearance of those in zoos and circuses is usually distressing. They rarely show any of the accepted signs of good health; in fact, the only healthy-looking zoo elephant I eves saw was at Durban, Natal; but there, of course, a supply of fresh green fodder is available.

I once suggested to one of the keepers of the elephants at the London Zoo that the poor condition of the animals was due to lack of sufficient green fodder. "Poor condition!" exclaimed he, indignantly, "what on earth are you talking about? The elephants are in perfect condition. And what do *you* know about it, anyhow?" "Well," said I, "I have been for many years in charge of a good number of elephants, and have had to do with dozens of others, so I feel that I do know a little bit about them." "And do you venture to assert," continued the keeper, "that any of your elephants are in healthier condition than ours?" "Well," said I, "if I had any elephants looking like that, I would shoot them to put them out of their misery."

After that, the keeper seemed to take a dislike to me, and the conversation languished.

I could go on for ever writing about elephants, which to me are the most interesting creatures in the world, but I fear that by this time some of my readers may be getting tired of them, so will switch over to describe a few queer humans.

XIII

Some Exotics

I said in the Preface to this book that almost all the inhabitants of Siam are of the Thai race. This is true, but there are several variations of Thai people, and the non-Thai inhabitants of the country make up in diversity for what they lack in numbers. It would be possible to collect together, within a hundred miles of the city of Chiengmai, at least fifteen different sorts of people, most of whom would be unable to understand one another's speech. Of Thai, there would be Siamese, Laos, Shans, Lus and Khons; and of non-Thai, there would be Meos, Yaos, Karens, Khamus, Lawas, Musus, and a few others, not to mention (if you could find them in the forest), Mrabris, or Phi Tong Luang.

It would be impossible, within the scope of this work, to give a full description of all these varying tribes. I will, therefore, confine myself to saying something about those who are either the most numerous or the most interesting.

For my information about the mountain tribes I am indebted to Mr. O. Gordon Young, who was actually born among them, and can speak several of their languages fluently.

THE MEO

There are two varieties of Meo [Hmong], their total number, according to Mr. Gordon Young's estimate, being 45,600. They are scattered all over northern Siam, building their villages at very high altitudes. They are not an indigenous people, but have immigrated from southern China within historical times, some fairly recently. They are divided into two sub-tribes, but these do not differ greatly from one another.

Until recently, the Meo, like many other hill tribes, lived mainly on the cultivation and sale of opium. Ever since the end of last century, this has been illegal, but until recent years the Siamese Government has made no serious attempt to suppress it. At the present time, many Meo villages grow maize or other crops.

The Meo are said to be very litigious among themselves, but do not, as a rule, have recourse to the Siamese courts or District Officers. When I visited a Meo village a good many years ago, I asked the Headman what they did in case of one of their number committing a crime. At first he denied that such a thing ever happened, but when I pressed him, he admitted that, some years before, one of his villagers had dug up a bag of rupees which a neighbour had buried under his hut. "Did you report that crime to the District Officer?" I asked. "Certainly not," the Headman replied. "We just took the culprit behind that tree and did like this"—here he drew his finger across his throat and uttered some very expressive gurgling sounds.

Until recently, the Meos were completely illiterate, but of late years the government has opened schools in many villages, and the border police do a great deal of educational work among the Meos and other hill tribes. As a consequence, they are becoming more and more sophisticated. I recently fell in with a young Meo who was wearing a white shirt, black trousers, shoes and socks, Panama hat, and wristwatch, and who was riding a bicycle! There is a Meo village only a few hours walk from Chiengmai, the inhabitants of which live mainly by posing for snapshots to the numerous tourists who now infest northern Siam.

The Meo are animists, sacrificing to the spirits of the streams and forests.

Meo women are often very attractive, having pink and white complexions. The men wear baggy trousers and blue and red turbans. The women wear pleated blue-and-white skirts, and walk with a swinging gait, rather like Scottish pipers.

They are not always very strict in their morals, and do not tend to repulse amorous advances by strangers. A young Lao I knew, a singularly stalwart and handsome young fellow, who went to peddle various trinkets in a Meo village, told me that the girls compelled him to stay there for several days, and that when he managed to break away, he could hardly walk down the mountain. "I never went there again," said he, "though I sold all my goods for very high prices. One can have too much of a good thing!"

Meo houses are built on the earth, usually of bamboo or other light materials. They often house, besides their owner, pigs, dogs, cats—and no doubt, a number of insect guests.

Their villages are usually more permanent than those of most of the hill tribes. They cultivate millet, sugar-cane, melons, pumpkins, potatoes, yam, flax, tobacco, and other crops. As they are apt to move their villages every few years, they do a lot of damage to the forests by felling all the large trees to start new plantations.

THE YAO

The Yao, like the Meos, are immigrants. They originate from South China, and many of them have come into Siam during the past century. There are at present seventy-five known Yao villages, mostly in Nan and Chiengrai provinces. In most respects they resemble the Meo, and their language, which has Chinese affinities, is like the Meo language, but the two tribes are not mutually intelligible.

The Yao are rather serious people, and do not go in much for music and dancing.

The Yao are clean people. They bathe daily, and are usually well dressed. The men wear blue home-spun baggy trousers, sometimes with coloured embroidery and silver buttons. They wear no headgear, but sometimes sport berets, which they buy in the towns.

They are skilful blacksmiths and silversmiths.

It may be said of both the Meo and the Yao that they are very superior people, judged by mountain standards. The men are strong and handsome, and the women often very beautiful. They show no antagonism to their Thai or other neighbours; but, on the other hand, they have no tendency towards amalgamation or absorption.

The total number of Yaos in Siam is given by Mr. Gordon Young as 10,000.

THE. LAWA

The Lawas are an interesting group of people for several reasons. Unlike most of the hill tribes, their ancestors came from the south, not from the north, and were possibly of Polynesian stock. They are related to the Wa of Burma, and settled in Siam in very ancient times, preceding not only the Thai, but also the Khmers.

The Wa of Burma were, until recent times, known as head-hunters, and it is likely that in ancient times the Lawa of Siam indulged in similar practices. When I lived at Singora, my Malay friends often spoke of northern Siam as a somewhat uncanny region, inhabited by murderous barbarians. This may be a lingering memory of the bad old days when the Lawa ruled the land, and when visitors from the south were likely to lose their heads—and perhaps be eaten.

At the present time, the Lawa are to be found mainly in the north-western regions of Siam. Their language does not resemble that of any of the other hill people except the Khamu, and almost all of them can speak Lao-Thai. Most of them are nominally Buddhists, but their Buddhism is rather a thin veneer and they go in for many animistic ceremonies, and practices. In appearance and dress they do not differ widely from their Thai neighbours, though their complexions are a shade darker.

Mr. Gordon Young estimates the number of Lawa in Siam at 9,000 at least.

THE KHAMU

The Khamu are immigrants from what is now called the Kingdom of Laos. Their language differs very widely from most of the languages and dialects of Mongolian origin. In particular, it possesses a letter "r" which is rolled in a manner to turn a Scotsman green with envy. The Lao, it is true, have an "r", but they never pronounce it.

Khamu villages are seldom built at altitudes of less than 2,500 feet. Their houses are well constructed and, unlike those of most other hill tribes, are built on posts.

The Khamu are for the most part animists, but those who have settled in or near towns or villages as a rule have become Buddhists.

Formerly there were not many Khamus in Siam, except those in mountain villages near the Laotian and Vietnam borders, but since the latter years of the last century, large numbers of Khamus have streamed into northern Siam to work in the teak forests. They were brought in by men whom they called their "Captains", who exploited them cruelly, and used to engage themselves as forest workers for periods of a year or more. Many of these forest workers married Lao wives, and have been absorbed into the Thai community.

I have never met any people so devoid of racial pride as the Khamus. They are always saying things like: "I can't do that. I am only a stupid Khamu", or "Do not expect too much from me. I am only a Khamu". They will cave in to a man much smaller than themselves, and explain that they cannot resist him, being "only Khamus". It is only when they settle down in Siam, adopt Thai dress, and marry Lao wives, that they begin to get rid of their inferiority complex, and forget that they are "only Khamus".

Mr. Gordon Young gives the number of Khamus as 3,300 but this number does not include the large number who have settled in towns and villages and married Lao wives.

THE KARENS

The Karens are, for the most part, immigrants from Burma. They inhabit the north-western regions of Siam, and are divided into four tribes, the Skaw Karen, the P'wo Karen, the B'ghwe Karen, and the Taungthu. They number in all 61,000.

These various tribes differ somewhat in their style of dress, but in language and customs there is not much diversity among them.

I will deal mainly with the Skaw Karen, who are the most numerous tribe.

These people are very attractive. Both men and women are strongly built, muscular and handsome. Both sexes smoke tobacco pipes and chew betel-nut.

Their language belongs to the Tibeto-Burman group, but most of the men and many of the women can speak Thai.

Most of them are animists by religion, but a good number of them are Christians—Baptists, to be precise.

Karen men wear short-sleeved red tunics, together with loose trousers, usually dark blue or black, and turbans of various shades. At present, they tend to abandon their tribal costumes in favour of the dress of their Lao-Thai neighbours.

Unmarried girls dress very simply, wearing merely a long, white slip-over, a tunic of coarse homespun cotton, with no embroidery. Married women wear an attractive short-sleeved dark blue blouse, with the lower part decorated with beautiful patterns, worked in red and white berries, which they use as beads.

In Burma, the Karens form a distinct state, and in the days of British rule were a very contented and peaceful community, but since Burma became independent, they have been in an almost constant state of rebellion, and large numbers of them have emigrated to Siam.

THE AKHA

The Akha tribes are to be found in the mountains to the extreme north of Siam. They are of Tibeto-Burman origin. Their language is tonal and monosyllabic. They are animists, and greatly dread evil spirits, holding frequent ceremonies for the purpose of driving them away.

They particularly fear water spirits, and for this reason seldom wash themselves. As a result, they are dirtier and more malodorous than other mountain tribes.

They will eat anything which is capable of being eaten, dogs, maggots, and many other creatures usually held to be "unclean".

They have some curious customs. For instance, they maintain in each group of villages a man, known as the "Ah Shaw", whose duty it is to prepare all the virgins for marriage by deflowering them at certain ceremonies each year.

All the men wear queues, and believe that they would go insane if they did not do so.

The women do most of the work, and children, too, are kept pretty busy. Women are very little valued.

The Akha are not old inhabitants of Siam, but have only immigrated into the country within the last thirty years or so. Their total number is estimated by Mr. Gordon Young at about 25,000.

They live largely by cultivating opium.

THE LAHU, OR MÜSÜ

Like the Akha, the Lahu are comparatively newcomers to Siam. They are divided into three tribes, the Lahu Sheleh, Lahu Shi and Lahu Nyi. These tribes dress somewhat differently, but all speak a similar language.

They are animists, and have a joss-house in each village where they sacrifice chickens and other small animals. The Lahu Nyi, and to some extent the Lahu Shi, believe in a so-called *man-god*. This person is a religious charlatan who lives in Burma, and who claims all sorts of magical powers.

Like so many hill people, all the Lahu depend chiefly on opium for their livelihood, and pay little attention to the laws of Siam prohibiting the cultivation of the opium poppy.

Mr. Gordon Young estimates the number of Lahu of all tribes at 15,000.

THE LISU

The Lisu are a Tibeto-Burman tribe, and are racially and linguistically allied to the Akha. There are about 17,300 of them in Siam, almost all living in the region immediately north of Chiengmai. Their villages are all at least 5,000 feet above sea-level.

The Lisu are fair-skinned people. Their average stature is higher than that of most other mountain people. Their men are strong, active and brave, and their women exceptionally beautiful.

The men wear double-breasted jackets, with silver buttons, loose, knee-length trousers, and navy turbans. The women wear very gaily embroidered coats, with quantities of silver ornaments, and enormous turbans. Like the men, they wear short, baggy trousers, and leggings or puttees.

The Lisu are animists. They live in continual fear of evil spirits, and, like the Akha, especially dread the spirits of the water.

They keep considerable numbers of livestock, ponies, pigs and chickens. But their main support consists in the cultivation of opium. They have, thus far, paid little attention to the laws forbidding opium growing.

THE MRABRI, YUMBRI, OR PHI TONG LUANG

Now I must say goodbye to the comparatively civilized hill tribes, with their more or less settled villages, their domestic animals, and their bright and gay garments, and ask you to visit with me some of the most primitive people in the whole world.

In former times, these forest dwellers were known as the *Phi Tong Luang,* or Spirits of the Yellow Leaves. This name was given to them because they were semi-nomadic, only building temporary huts of leaves which they abandoned when the leaves turned yellow. The word "phi", or spirit, shows that there was felt to be something mysterious about them. Until recent times it was widely believed that no such people existed, but that they were merely a "native superstition". They ranked with the Loch Ness Monster and the Abominable Snowman as creatures whose very existence was the subject of controversy.

The mystery was unveiled in the year 1936, when Professor Hugo Adolf Bernatzik, an Austrian anthropologist, and his wife, spent some weeks in a forest north of Nan, in close proximity to a community of these elusive folk, and wrote a book describing their habits and customs, and showing a number of charming photographs. Even then, some hardened sceptics were unconvinced, and ventured to cast doubts on the bona-fides of Professor and Mrs. Bernatzik. Within the past two years these pioneers have been triumphantly vindicated by Mr. Kraisri Nimmanhaeminda, a well-known Thai banker and industrialist, who has conducted two expeditions to a region about twenty miles from that visited by the Bernatziks, and had several meetings with the members of a community of forest-dwellers.

Doubts have been raised as to whether the people described by Dr. Bernatzik and those met by Mr. Kraisri are the same. Dr. Bernatzik gives their name as Yumbri, Mr. Kraisri as Mrabri, and the vocabularies drawn up by these two investigators differ widely. However, Dr. Bernatzik's vocabulary was compiled under very unfavourable conditions. He himself did not speak English well, and he had to work through a Thai-English intermediary and after him a whole chain of interpreters.

On Mr. Kraisri's second expedition, he was accompanied by Mr. J. J. Boeles, photographer, and Dr. G. Flatz, M.D., of Bonn. They met twenty-four Mrabri at a spot in the forest arranged by a go-between. They did not go to the Mrabri camp, and consequently met only one woman, an aged crone in poor health, who probably came in the hope of obtaining medicine. Eighteen of the men underwent very thorough physical examinations.

The Mrabri men are of short stature, but of sturdy and graceful build. They are not very shy or unfriendly, and were easily persuaded to undergo physical examinations, also to sing and dance for their visitors.

Their origin is uncertain. They may be aborigines, or they may be immigrants dating from more or less modern times. It is also possible that there are several groups, of varying origin. The name Mrabri means *Forest Men.*

The Mrabri do not build houses, but merely rough shelters. They do not go in for agriculture, have no knowledge of weaving or pottery, and wear no ornaments. They do not use money, but obtain what they need from the outer world by bartering forest products for rice, salt and cloth.

Their clothing is extremely scanty. Some authorities assert that they go naked when not in contact with strangers.

They are animists, and believe in good and bad spirits. Many of them are tattooed with cabalistic signs, but these are done for them by outsiders. They are capable of counting up to twenty, but do not reckon their ages by years, and only judge time by the position of the sun.

The Mrabri have some artistic taste. They are able to plait rattan mats in very pleasing patterns, and to make bags of attractive design. They also know how to forge knives and spearheads.

The diet of the Mrabri is very restricted. They do not eat rice regularly. Their staple diet is roots, yams, nuts, bulbs, wild fruit and vegetables; also the meat of such small animals as they can catch without traps. They also collect wild honey. Now and then they obtain, by barter, a pig from the Meo.

The Mrabri are extraordinarily musical. They can sing, chant and dance, and some of them can play on the flute. They are very skilful at improvising verses. This is an English version of one of their songs.

Mrabri Song

Which of us is to go to sleep,
    Passing before the other?
Sing a song of the forest deep,
    Sing of the wilds, my brother.
We know nought of the tricks of trade,
    We know nought of the city,
Fighting the forest, deep in the glade,
    My Lord, we crave your pity!
Please, My Lord, wild men are we,
    We are ready your slaves to be.

Where I can set my two feet down,
    That is my real home;
You, who dwell in the distant town,
    Pray be my friend, pray come!
Talk to me now, teach me to think,
    Seek not to cross that hill,
Sit with me by the streamlet's brink,
    Stay and hark to me still;
Stay and listen, for night is nigh,
    Noi, noi, noitae, noitae, hai!

XIV

Miscellaneous

I have heard some foreigners accuse the Siamese of bad manners. Nothing could be more unjust. The Siamese possess the most perfect natural good manners in the world. As for the alleged good manners of arbitrary convention, naturally their standards differ in some respects from ours, as ours do from theirs.

For instance, English and American people of the more cultured classes rather dislike spitting in public, but in Siam there is not much prejudice against this habit. Until comparatively recent times, the chewing of betel-nut was very widely indulged in, and this rendered it necessary for people to keep on spitting at very frequent intervals. Spittoons were among the most prominent household utensils, and a gold spittoon even formed part of the regalia of Siam. If you paid a visit to an old-fashioned Siamese house, a spittoon of generous proportions was usually placed beside you as soon as you sat down; sometimes two were provided, or even three—one on each side, and a small one on the table for use in emergency.

Chewing is not a common habit now, and the cultivation of the betel-nut—or, more correctly, the areca nut—is only carried on in a small way. Siamese and Lao of the younger generation usually have the most beautiful white teeth, but when I first came to the country white teeth were so rare as to be looked upon as an eccentricity; to foreigners those black mouths appeared repulsive, but the Siamese did not regard them as a disfigurement.

In former times, when I was entertaining Siamese guests of old-fashioned tastes, who did not like to go too long without their betel-nut, I always had a supply ready for them. On one occasion I had prepared a beautiful chewing outfit, spittoon included, and had told my servant, a new and raw lad, that he would find the betel-tray and the spittoon in the bedroom, and that he must bring them into the drawing-room and place them near our distinguished Siamese guest as soon as we had finished dinner. When the time came, the boy brought along the betel-tray all right, but instead of the spittoon he imported from the bedroom a utensil of an altogether different sort, not usually seen in drawing-rooms, and plonked it down boldly in the midst of the assembled company. Some of the ladies eyed it askance, but I thought it best to make light of the matter, so I merely remarked: "Not that one, boy, please. The other one—without a handle."

I found that some absurdly insular English people, who were upset by the sight of excessive chewing and spitting, were often apt to overlook the fact that they themselves were causing offence by some action which appeared quite harmless to them. For instance, crossing the legs. It is not thought polite in Siam to cross the legs when speaking to people of good position; still worse is it to point one's toe at them. A Siamese lady of high rank once complained to me that a certain Englishman had treated her with gross discourtesy. As I knew him for one of the politest of men, I expressed surprise, whereupon she explained as follows:

"Not only did he keep his legs crossed the whole time he was talking to me, but he even pointed his right toe at me; and what is more, he *waggled* it!"

True politeness, of course, is something far removed from such trifles as spitting or toe-waggling. Are not generosity and hospitality symptoms of genuine good manners? If this be so, the Siamese, of all ranks, are among the best-mannered people in the world. They give generously to all public and charitable objects, and they are ready to show true hospitality towards almost anyone at any time. It is wonderful to see how even the poorest people will accord one a cordial and cheerful welcome into their houses, however unexpected the visit, and how they will bustle around to find a mat for one to sit on, a cushion for one to lean against, and to provide tea and such dainties as are available. In country places, most householders are always ready to allow strangers passing through their village to sleep in their houses for a night or two.

Another delightful thing in Siam used to be the jolly way in which passers-by used to greet one another. This custom is, alas! not so common in these days of so-called culture; but even now, there are still plenty of people who are always ready with a pleasant smile and a friendly remark for anyone they may chance to meet.

We English are rather secretive, and dislike questions about our personal affairs. In Siam, personal questions are held to show a kindly interest. The commonest greeting is, "Where are you going?" and if you engage in conversation with a stranger you will probably be asked your age, the nature of your job, the amount of your salary, and the number and sex of your children. This is not a sign of idle curiosity, and the enquirer probably does not really want to know how much you are paid, but such queries show a friendly interest in your affairs. To be offended would be ridiculous—and it is not essential to give correct answers.

Some foreign ladies are taken aback when asked to state their ages in public; a foolish prejudice, from which Siamese ladies seem to be exempt. I may add that it is quite useless for a lady to understate her age; if she does do, she may quite likely be told, politely but frankly, that she looks far more than the age she has given. People in Siam do not try to make themselves out to be younger than their real ages. On the contrary, many people, especially men of the poorer classes, devote some attention to the task of growing as old as possible as quickly as they can manage it. I fancy that this tendency dates from the days when certain taxes were not levied on men who had reached the age of sixty, or who were less than twenty years old. In those days, it was natural that as soon as a man was twenty one of his chief objects in life was to reach the age of sixty by some sort of short cut, and all kinds of ingenious devices were resorted to with this end in view. We had one servant who sprang from the age of nineteen to thirty-two in three days. Shan immigrants often tried to induce the British Consul to put down perfectly absurd ages on their registration certificates, which they then hoped to work off on the Siamese poll-tax collector as documentary proof of the matter. Fifty-eight was the favourite age for Shans. To put down sixty and claim exemption right away might arouse nasty suspicions; but the bogus fifty-eighter paid his tax for that year and got a Siamese receipt bearing that age; and so again the next year. He then possessed two Siamese and one British official document to support his claim to tax exemption the third year. I soon discovered this dodge, and from that time always assessed the ages of Shans myself: I probably knew as much about it as they did, anyhow.

Quite apart from wily, tax-dodging motives, country people in Siam tend to exaggerate their ages. To begin with, they count their ages from the time of conception rather than of birth; moreover, they reckon by complete years, not months, so that a person who has lived through part of three years is three years old, even though he may have only seen a few days of the first and third years.

Official registration of births is of comparatively recent introduction, and is not even now universally enforced, but in northern Siam a family register is kept on strips of palm leaf. People do not much like producing these palm strips, as an exact knowledge of the day and hour of a man's birth may be put to evil use by witches and sorcerers. However, when administering the estates of British subjects I often had to insist on being shown these certificates in confidence, as otherwise young folk of seventeen or eighteen would claim property to which they were not entitled until the age of twenty-one. I never met with a single case in which the age was not over-stated by a year at least, often by two or three, and in most instances without any intention of deceiving me.

In Siam, people often tend to be a bit indefinite about other things besides their ages. In England, if a man be asked: "Why did you do that?" and replies: "I did," he will be thought both uninformative and uncivil. In Siam, such a reply seems to be thought quite reasonable. "Why did you not do as I told you?" "I did not, Sir." "Why did you polish my brown shoes with black polish?" "I did, Sir." "Why were you drunk last night?" "I was, Sir." All these answers are sound, natural and logical, and if you cannot accept them as such, that is your own fault.

I once knew a man who refused to have anything to do with such replies as these; he would yell at his servants for reasons, *reasons,* REASONS, until at last, in desperation, they would produce what they thought he wanted; and then he would tear their poor little reasons to shreds and demand better ones. His health broke down in the end, and he had to return to Europe.

As for me, I early realised that to refuse to accept mere admissions as reasons would land me in a hospital or a lunatic asylum; so I accepted them, but in doing so I made a mental reservation to the effect that I was conceding something to a national idiosyncracy, and that in actual fact admissions were *not* reasons. I now realise that admissions really *are* reasons, but it took me thirty-five and a half years to reach this point. I doubt whether any Englishman could do it in less, though an Irish friend of mine managed it in seventeen and a quarter years; but he came from Cork.

Little peculiarities such as this are very upsetting to nervous and irritable foreigners in Siam, and sometimes lead them to strike or beat their servants. They forget for the moment how mean it is to strike a man who can hardly be expected to hit back, and perhaps do not realise how vulgar their action appears to their Siamese friends. An Englishman to whom I once said this urged, in reply, that the Siamese themselves are not always averse to the infliction of corporal punishment on their subordinates. On thinking this over, I realised that a Siamese of good position does not, as a rule, strike or cuff an inferior; if he wants such a thing done, he gets it done for him by somebody else. The infliction of corporal punishment is a low and menial job, which a gentleman ought not to do for himself.

I do not think the Siamese feel quite such a hatred and loathing of corporal punishment as the Malays do, but they greatly dislike being beaten or even touched by a rattan, which is reserved for criminals; even worse than this is to be struck or touched with a broom—this is really something frightful.

Another thing which Siamese and Lao servants do not at all like is to have anything thrown at them. I do not mean thrown violently—to that, of course, anyone would object— but thrown carelessly or in an offhand manner. For instance, most men who have earned a tip would rather go without it than have a coin or note thrown towards them. In Siam, things must be handed from one person to another in a decent and civil manner. In giving anything to a superior, two hands ought to be used, even though one hand only takes a formal part in the matter, by touching the other elbow.

A Siamese sometimes apologises to you if, in the course of conversation, he has occasion to refer to his leg, foot or stomach. This degree of delicacy appears excessive to us, especially as objects and subjects can be publicly referred to which are usually very much veiled among Europeans and Americans. For instance, clinical details as to complaints of both sexes are sometimes referred to in mixed company in a way which rather embarrasses us.

But of course all this sort of thing is purely conventional, and I dare say we shock the Siamese much oftener than they do us. The peculiar nature of their language, with its system of tones, rarely mastered by foreigners, is full of snares and pitfalls for the unwary. I remember once hearing a Prince ask an English lady where she had been. She put on her sweetest smile, mustered her best Siamese accent, and replied—as she thought—"I have been out riding." What she actually said was that she had been to the "lavatory",—but in terms far too coarse for me to reproduce here.

Translations are always tricky things. A friend of mine once received an invitation to an official function, bearing in one corner the note: "Evening dress with decorations." His clerk translated it for him thus: "Nightdress with ribbons."

The Siamese and Laos are more tolerant in regard to religious matters than any other people in the world. They have always admitted foreign missionaries to their shores, and have even encouraged and assisted them in many ways. The first Roman Catholic missionaries to land in Siam were Portuguese; they came in the reign of Rama Thibodi II (1491–1529) and were permitted by that monarch to erect a large crucifix in a public place in his capital. His broad-minded example has been followed by every king of Siam since, if we except Phetraja (1688–1703). This king is usually considered to have persecuted the Roman Catholics, but the so-called persecution was in reality a political move against the French, whose influence had become very great under the preceding king. Phetraja was a usurper, set up by the anti-French party, and he did not persecute any Christians other than those of French nationality. It may thus fairly be said that Christians, *qua* Christians, have seldom been persecuted in Siam. A noble record indeed, especially when we call to mind all the racks and thumbscrews, iron boots, halters, axes, stakes and faggots so freely and so blasphemously used in Europe in the name of Him who bade us love one another. It is a tragic fact that those who profess to follow the religion of love have always been the cruellest and bloodiest persecutors.

When travelling in the north of Siam it is very usual for the wayfarer to spend a night in a Buddhist temple. In fact every temple contains, somewhere in its precincts, one or more buildings for the accommodation of passers-by. Moreover, if any fastidious traveller does not care for the temple rest-house, the priests will often allow him to sleep in the main temple building—the church or chapel containing the images of Buddha. All that they ask is that the self-invited guest shall not offend their feelings by bathing in the temple, or by killing fowls or other living creatures within the sacred precincts. They have even been known to curtail their evening prayers out of pity for some extra weary wayfarer.

Try to imagine an English rector inviting a party of hikers to camp out in his church, sleep in the aisle, and dine in the vestry!

I like the Siamese way best. Just as Buddha provides a refuge for men's weary souls, so do his earthly temples give rest and refreshment to tired bodies, and by so doing forfeit neither dignity nor holiness. Quite the reverse.

The orthodox Buddhist ideal is that every man shall become a priest for some portion of his life, and in former times a very large number actually did so. In the south it was, and is, usual for a man, if ordained at all, to become a full priest; in the north it is more customary for lads to be ordained as novices, resign when they grow up, and never take the full vows. But both in the north and the south the rush and strain of modern life has rendered it impossible of late years for most boys and men to find time even for a short period in a Buddhist temple. The government has been compelled, moreover, to institute certain tests and restrictions on candidates for ordination, in order to prevent the temples from becoming refuges for tax-dodgers and evaders of military service. Before this was done, it now and then happened that, when a village Headman was called upon to compile a list of the young men in his village who were liable for conscription, he was compelled to report that there were none at all, but that the local temple had put up several temporary buildings to accommodate the abnormal number of young priests and novices.

The practice of shaving the heads and eyebrows of priests was originally instituted so as to render them unattractive, and therefore less liable to be assailed by the temptations of the flesh. In fact, the lack of hair and eyebrows is not always a disfigurement. It seems to fit in with the yellow robe, and actually to improve the appearance of some men. However this may be, the standard of morality among Buddhist priests and novices in Siam is remarkably high. The number of priests is very great, and the Siamese are a warm-blooded race, but the occurrence of scandals affecting the priesthood is extremely rare.

The Siamese idea of beauty differs in some respects from ours. They particularly admire a fair complexion, and it is difficult to get them to admit that a lady is pretty if she has an unusually dark skin. The ladies who win beauty prizes in Siam do not always appeal to European taste.

Siamese women are completely emancipated. Polygamy is no longer officially recognised, though it is still pretty openly practised by men who can afford it. In fact, the new marriage laws exist more on paper than in actuality; for instance, very few people outside the larger cities go to the trouble of registering their marriages with their District Officer.

Women's rights are well safeguarded. A married woman seems to possess greater rights over her husband's property than is the case in England; in fact, she usually claims a share in everything he owns. Women carry on a great part of the business of the country, and there are now women barristers, doctors, dentists, chauffeuses; there is even one lady member of Parliament. As for business, I do not doubt their capacity in that direction, but now and then I have found them just a tiny bit difficult to deal with.

In southern Siam, when a man marries he usually still goes on existing as a distinct human being. In the north, there is a certain tendency to regard him as a sort of domestic animal belonging to his mother-in-law. He is expected, as a rule, to live with her, and if she be of an overbearing disposition, as she often is, she may well make his life a burden to him. It is terrible to think how few Lao couples there are who can have a nice, comfortable little domestic row all to themselves, and then kiss and make friends again. At the first hard words between them, mother-in-law takes a hand, and by the time she has finished—if she ever *does* finish— they have probably decided on a divorce. Again and again I have begged and implored young British subjects who have married into Lao families, and who have sought my advice after a domestic dispute, to go away somewhere, anywhere, with their wives, provided that it is somewhere where there are no mothers-in-law. Often the young wife dared not do anything so original, so the old lady talked them asunder; but if they managed to break away, all was well. If all ladies in northern Siam were compelled, at their daughters' weddings, to take a vow of absolute silence for a period of two years, the number of divorces would be enormously decreased.

A young Shan I once knew married a very rich Lao girl, and went to live with her in a house containing her mother, grandmother, three aunts, two great-aunts and an elderly female cousin. Her young brother, aged about sixteen, was the only other male creature on the premises. I suggested to the bridegroom, before the wedding, that he might find things a bit harassing; but he said that the family was so rich that he was prepared to put up with a goodish deal. However, he did a bolt in exactly three weeks, taking his young brother-in-law with him; they went to work as coolies on the railway, and never returned home again. The wife, mother-in-law, grandmother, aunts, great-aunts and female cousin are, I am sure, still talking about the baseness and ingratitude of the male sex.

When this young fellow first ran away, his mother-in-law came to see me about it. I told her that I had no power to force him to return, and delicately hinted that I might have been tempted to run away myself, had I been in his place. She was very angry with me, and told me that it was a public scandal that I, as British Consul-General, should condone such atrocious wickedness. Finally, she warned me that she would write and tell King George V all about me. I often wonder whether she really did so. It is marvellous that her son-in-law was able to bear her for three weeks—not to mention the grandmother, aunts, great-aunts and female cousin.

I once read somewhere a funny joke about the courage of a polygamist in taking on several mothers-in-law. This is not really a joking matter at all, but deadly serious. I know all about it, for though I myself only ever had one mother-in-law (and a comparatively amenable one) I have had to administer the estates of several men who had a remarkably good supply. It is appalling, when trying to make a fair division of a dead man's property, to have five or six widows to pacify, each widow usually bringing her mother, and often an aunt or two, to lend moral and vocal support to her claims.

There seems to be no good reason why fathers-in-law should not be just as important a vital force in the world as mothers-in-law. All I can say is that they are not. I can do anything with fathers-in-law; they will eat, so to speak, out of my hand. When I was called in to arbitrate in a family dispute, I always used to beg that the fathers-in-law might be trotted out for me to deal with; but it was very rarely considered safe to let me interview them alone, and without feminine supervision.

Probably women, of all races, pay more attention to details than men do. Men reckon in pounds or dollars, or ticals, women in farthings or cents or stangs. In Siam, a contempt for detail is very marked in many of the men, especially details regarding time and distance. In northern Siam it is a serious thing, when travelling, to have to ask for any information about the way. If you ask how far off a place is, you are generally told, "*Baw paw kai*". This expression, which is supposed to mean "Not very far", is in reality the concentrated essence of indefiniteness, and to the initiated conveys no meaning whatever. It may mean half a mile or it may mean twenty miles. I have never heard it used to mean a thousand miles, but I daresay it may mean that too. If you probe the matter further, your informant will silently point to a part of the sky, signifying: "When the sun reaches that spot, you will have reached your destination." When you *do* reach your destination, the sun, if it has not set, is never anywhere near the spot indicated.

Another strange thing about finding one's way in northern Siam is that guides who are engaged on a daily wage to show one the way quite often do not know it themselves. On one occasion I engaged two guides at a tical a day each, as one refused to travel alone. At about ten o'clock the first morning they both sat down beside a stream and said: "You must camp here. There is no more water for six or seven hours' march ahead." As the day was hot, and I had elephants with me, I was about to follow their advice, when a man happened to come along from the other direction. I asked him about the matter, and he assured me that there was a small stream just over the next hill. On we went. When we reached the small stream, both the guides sat down and again assured me that there was no more water for six hours' march ahead. This time I refused to believe them, and said that I meant to cross the next hill, come what might. We did so and in a short time came to a large stream, along which we travelled for thirty miles, crossing it that day thirty-two times, and the next day eighty-seven times! The guides explained that they had forgotten all about that stream. Of course, they still expected to be paid for their services, and to add to the irony of the situation, one of them developed fever and had to ride an elephant, and another got a sore leg, on which I had to put oinment and bandages every morning and evening. When we got to the end of the journey, they both seemed quite grieved at having to part from me, saying that they had found it a great pleasure to travel in my company, and hoped that next time I needed guides I would engage them again. And what is more, they looked as though they meant it.

Another time, I asked a Siamese District Officer to find me a guide. He kindly did so, but after a few wanderings along side tracks, the guide admitted to me that he had never in all his life been on that road before. "Why, then," I enquired, "did you allow me to engage you as a guide?" "Well, Sir," said he, "the District Officer asked me to go with you, and as I am a humble person, it would ill befit me to argue with a District

Officer." "But do you expect me to pay you? " I pursued. "Well," said he, sadly, "I don't want much, but I am a poor man, and it would ill befit you to give me nothing." But that time I was firm, and I paid him nothing at all. I am sure that to this day he remembers me as a sort of robber.

These guide incidents are rather symptomatic of a tendency which exists among the Laos to undertake any kind of job, hoping to worry through somehow. A man with a very rudimentary knowledge of motor engineering will blithely dismantle a car, and will feel rather hurt when the wretched thing refuses to be reassembled so easily. Moreover, a man of very poor physique will sometimes undertake to do heavy work far beyond his strength, and will honestly try to do it, and feel very ashamed when he fails.

As a matter of fact, a great many Siamese and Lao men really can do a large variety of different things, and may be called rather versatile as compared with their English or American opposite numbers. For instance, almost everybody can do some gardening, sewing or cooking. In England or America, if you were to request the average chauffeur or gardener to cook, say, a four-course dinner, he would probably phone for the nearest mental specialist to come and have a look at you. In Siam he would quietly get three bricks and a bundle of twigs, and would set to work to cook the dinner. Quite possibly the result would be hardly equal to the fare provided at the Cecil or the Ritz, but would be more or less eatable.

The same with carpentry. Almost everyone is a carpenter, and the articles produced by amateurs in this line are often surprisingly good.

As for building houses, of course anyone can do that. Any man of ordinary intelligence can build himself a nice little timber house, with a tiled roof; and when it comes to bamboo houses with thatched roofs—well, even the village idiot can build one of those.

Bamboo houses thatched with grass or leaves spring up in a moment, and very pretty and delightful many of them are.

There are also some all-bamboo houses, even the roof being made of split sections of bamboo.

I once came upon a little all-bamboo house built by some of the railroad coolies when the northern line was under construction, and went into it to shelter from a shower of rain. The posts of it were of bamboo, the floor was bamboo, and the walls, windows, doors and roof were all made of bamboo. In it I found a fire of bamboo chips, near which, seated on a bamboo stool, a man was cooking something savoury in a pot made of a section of bamboo.

"What are you cooking there?" I asked.

"Bamboo," said he.

XV

The Bamboo House

Writing about bamboo houses in the previous chapter re-
minded me of the little bamboo house we bought a few years ago.

I fear that I am about to write a short story, which I ought
not to do, because this is only a book of reminiscences and
anecdotes. Moreover, I know that I cannot write short stories
at all well. I know it because I once wrote several of them. I
thought they were beautiful little stories, so I sent them round
to the editors of all the magazines in England, and one in
Scotland, but in every case they were returned to me as being
quite unfit for publication. I do not mean that they were
improper; they were just no good. So now you know what to
expect, and if you are in a critical mood, you had better not
bother to read this chapter.

Our bamboo house cost us, in English money, only about
£5. We bought it second-hand and had to pay another ten
shillings to do it up and re-erect it in our compound. It was,
and is, a splendid little house. It contains a living verandah, a
small bedroom, and a kitchen. It is built entirely of bamboo,
except for the roof, which is made of dried leaves. We bought
it for a servant of ours named Sing Keo—Crystal Lion. He
lived with his cousin just up the road, and he asked us to buy
him a bamboo house, so that he would not have so far to come
to work. So we bought it, and what is more, we helped to
furnish it. In the bedroom it had a large straw mat; on top of
this was a mattress, over which hung a mosquito net ; there
was also a small table, with a looking-glass. In the verandah

there were a table, two chairs, a stool, and a striped mat. On the wall, in the post of honour, were four pictures; one of King George VI, in naval uniform, one of the King of Siam, in military uniform, one of myself, in Consular uniform, and one of my wife, in a hammock. There were also a few pictures of ordinary people. In the kitchen there were four pots and a pan, one dish, six plates and three cups, two knives, two forks and two spoons.

We asked Sing Keo whether he would like us to buy him a cradle too. He looked shy, and said: "Not yet." But of course, when a young fellow of twenty asks for a bamboo house all to himself, one knows what to expect. Moreover, Sing Keo had been practising sentimental airs on his little wooden banjo for weeks past, and every evening he had been going out alone, banjo in hand—and he always went in the same direction.

We knew that Sing Keo would marry a nice girl, and so he did. She made her appearance only a week after Sing Keo had taken over the bamboo house, and her name was Ta Nin— Sapphire Eye. She was only eighteen years old, and had been brought up in the American Mission School, so that not only could she read and write, but could wash and sew as well. Best of all, she was an orphan, so Sing Keo was able to bring her to live with him in his own little house, and had no nagging mother-in-law to worry him.

Sing Keo had a buffalo, which sometimes slept near the bamboo house at night. He himself had no time to plough his little field, being busy with our work, but during the padi season his brother took the buffalo and did his ploughing for him, calling incessantly, "Kwa, kwa" (Right, right). He never called out, "Left, left," for buffaloes have a string in their left nostril, so a little pull or jerk will send them that way; but for a right turn, one has to yell, "Kwa, kwa!"

The buffalo was fat, and there was also a fat dog named Deng, which lived in the verandah of the bamboo house, and was supposed to scare off any thieves who might come to steal the buffalo, or perhaps even the pictures of King George, the

King of Siam, my wife and myself. Poor Deng was a nervous dog, and I do not think he would ever have dared to bite anybody. Whenever I spoke to him, he trembled like the proverbial aspen leaf.

There was a little spirit which helped to guard the bamboo house. It lived in a tiny shrine by the river bank, and was fed on bananas, little snacks of meat, and all sorts of dainties such as spirits like.

Almost a year went by—a happy year for Sing Keo and his young wife—and then we thought it was time to renew our offer of a cradle. They accepted it, and before long there was a plump baby boy sleeping in it. His name was Ai Tep— little angel—and he was like his mother, but a little bit like Sing Keo too. They thought he was the nicest baby in the world, but they were careful never to say so, for that would have been very unlucky; and of course we never said so, though we were inclined to agree with them, now that our own babies were babies no longer.

Sing Keo had not given up playing his banjo when he married, and now he found a new use for it—to lull Ai Tep to sleep: and very efficacious it was.

Two more happy years went by, in the bamboo house. Ai Tep could run about and play, and was big enough to tease the fat dog, and almost big enough to ride the fat buffalo. He slept no more in the cradle, not because he was too big for it, but because it was being got ready for a new tenant.

Then, one morning at two, we were awakened by the voice of Sing Keo calling: "Nai, Nai; Mem, Mem, forgive me for waking you. Ta Nin is very ill." We got up and heard from him how "the baby did not want to be born", and how the Lao doctor did not know what to do, and said that Ta Nin would die. So we sent for the Mission doctor. He had only just gone to bed—where doctors are few, they sleep when they can—but he came along at once, as we knew he would, and took Ta Nin away to the hospital. Sing Keo prayed to his little spirit, and my wife prayed to the Great Spirit, but neither of them did anything about it and indeed if spirits, great or small, were influenced by our prayers for the sick, then Death, though it would be a rare event, would be very terrible, for none but the utterly unloved would ever die.

So when the morning came, Sing Keo returned all alone to the bamboo house, while his wife and his baby daughter lay dead in the hospital. He took down all his pictures and put them away in a box, together with his banjo, and he gave to his brother his furniture and plates and dishes and pots and pans, and he took away his little son Ai Tep, and his fat buffalo and his dog Deng, and left them at his brother's house away across the padi fields; and he himself went to live with his cousin up the road, and came to work every morning, just as he had done before we bought the bamboo house for him.

As for the bamboo house, we bought it back from Sing Keo for half price, for, as we pointed out to him, we were richer than he, and as we had given it to him outright, it would not be proper for us to take it back for nothing.

My wife and I were often asked by other servants to let them live in the bamboo house, but we always refused. So there it stood empty. But we kept it in good repair, even down to the little spirit shrine, and had it cleaned and swept now and then, for we hoped to find a tenant for it some day.

***

Two years have gone by since Ta Nin died. It is spring, which means, in Siam, the end of the hot weather, not of the cold. The first rains have fallen, and the parched lawns and scorched trees are putting on their new green garments. And not only the vegetable world; for three days past Sing Keo has been wearing a beautiful new green silk shirt, and a smart new pair of trousers; and what is more, he has been practising his banjo, which we had not heard since Ta Nin's time. And yesterday he asked for leave to go out to the padi field and bring back his little son to stay with him.

While he was away, my wife and I prepared a surprise for him, and when he came back we took him quietly over to the bamboo house, and showed it to him all swept and garnished, with a new mattress and mosquito net, new chairs and mats, and a new kitchen outfit. And we told him that we had been keeping it for him, and begged him to come back and live in it again—with his wife. Sing Keo wept a little, and laughed a little, and asked us whether we thought it wrong of him to marry again. And of course we answered: "No, you are right. You loved your little wife and were good to her, but fate took her from you. You are young, and must live out your life on earth like other men, not as a lonely widower. You need a wife to look after you, and poor little Ai Tep needs a mother."

"But how did you find out about it?" asked Sing Keo.

"How did we find out?" we replied; "why of course we knew it as soon as we heard the sound of your banjo; and we were glad to hear that sound, for it told us that you had overcome your sorrow."

The fat dog Deng is dead, so we have given Sing Keo a new dog—a fox terrier pup. As I sit here, I can see little Ai Tep playing with the pup on the grass in front of the bamboo house, while his father is busy inside—busy hanging up the pictures of King George, of the King of Siam, and of my wife and myself. And when he has finished that job, I have promised to help him repair the spirit shrine.

So, you see, the story of the bamboo house is a stupid story, like all my other stories which all the editors in England—and one in Scotland—said were no good. It is only about everyday, stale old things; love and happiness, death and sorrow—and hope. There is nothing of the "mysterious East" about such commonplace things; they are the same everywhere, whether in big marble palaces or little bamboo houses.

If you did not like my story, do not blame me. I warned you. And now I must say goodbye. Sing Keo has come down from the bamboo house, and is waiting for me to help him repaint the little spirit shrine.

Afterword

William Alfred Rae Wood provided some biographical notes about himself in an earlier edition of *Consul in Paradise*, the preface to which amplifies some of the information. He tells us he was born in Blundell Sands, Liverpool, in 1878, and his father was a partner in a firm with an office in Greece, where he had been born. Wood junior was the sixth of eight children, and the only boy. His father opened an office in Bruges, where the family went to live. At the age of twelve, young William entered Dulwich College as a day-boy and apparently enjoyed his time there. In 1893 he was sent to Switzerland to improve his Belgian French, and then studied in Germany. In 1895 he was in England again, preparing for the examination of British Consular Service for student interpreters in the Far East. He was successful, and became a student interpreter in Siam at the age of eighteen in June 1898.

He was to serve some 35 years in Siam, stationed in Bangkok, Chiang Mai, Chiang Rai, Nan, Lampang and Songkhla, rising in position to be consular assistant, vice-, and consul-general. His first up-country posting was to Nan in 1905, as vice-consul. His last posting was in 1913 to Chiang Mai where he stayed until his retirement as long ago as 1931, by when he was consul-general. He was to spend more time in retirement in Siam than in active life, but kept himself busy with his garden in his estate at Nong Hoi, close to his beloved Chiang Mai, with his memoirs as we have them here, with writing short stories, and teaching English to young Thai men, "a very interesting occupation, and, I like to think, not entirely useless."

He tells us he met his wife, Boon (Panya Chitpreecha) of Shan descent, in 1906 and married her the same year; the couple had two daughters. In his spare time, he compiled what was for many years a standard work, *The History of Siam*. D.K. Wyatt, author of the standard *Thailand: A Short History* (1984: 321) wrote of this: "A few intrepid souls have attempted to write general histories [of Thailand]. The first was W.A.R.Wood, *A History of Siam* (London, 1926; reprint Bangkok, 1959), which covered the Bangkok period in just eight pages and is now badly outdated." Furthermore, modern scholarship looks askance at works which do not give sources for information provided.

During the war, as an enemy alien, he was interned for rather more than three years in Bangkok, but never wrote about and chose not to speak of that period. He died on 21 January 1970 aged 91 and was buried in the Chiang Mai Foreign Cemetery. His wife, in failing health, sold their property in 1979 and went to live in Dorchester in England with her surviving daughter Amala Rose. She died there aged 92 in November 1982, and her ashes were brought back to Thailand and interred next to her husband.

Much of Wood's consular time seems to have been spent in settling legal disputes involving British subjects (those were the days when consuls had their own courts, and subjects included Indians, Burmese, Malays, Hong Kong and Singapore Chinese and many others, as well as straightforward Brits), and held various legal positions in addition to his consular ones. The British Legation in Bangkok had its own jail (and its own gallows). The consular courts were gradually replaced by International Courts, where Thai judges sat with foreign legal advisors and the British consul could attend relevant cases and give an opinion. The International Courts were finally dissolved in 1925. Though untrained as a lawyer, Wood obviously enjoyed his legal work (and had a healthy contempt for the letter rather than the spirit of the law), and many of the stories here are derived from disputes which came before him.

Consul in Paradise first appeared in 1935 under the title *Land of Smiles*. By 1965, this cliché was so overdone that the new title was felicitous, even if it has echoes of an earlier work, *An Asian Arcady: The Land and Peoples of Northern Siam* (Cambridge, 1926), by Reginald Le May, who was another person who fell under the spell of what is now often called Lan Na. It also fully captures the mood of distant days in distant lands, seen through the eyes of an old man reminiscing. It has enormous charm, and some incidents—like the Danish police officer popping the severed nose and upper lip of the wife of an Indian national (and thus juridically British) into his glass of whisky as he and Wood sat chatting and the severed flesh and knife were produced by the plaintiff—remain in the memory for a long time.

Those who like a well-ordered volume may not approve of the casual raconteur style and assembling of recalled incidents. We start off with memoirs of Wood's early days in the consulate in Bangkok, a place of fires, pawnshops, pony races on the Pramane Ground, Indian watchmen, gambling dens, and DBSs ("Distressed British Subjects"), old-time penniless and sponging backpackers, the bane of consular officials). Wood is quite capable of the occasional off-colour remark, as when quoting the captain of the Russian gunboat who informed everyone willing to listen "I am here wid der *Askold*. But I have der varm heart."

In his account of the courts, he belongs to the school maintaining the law is an ass, and notes "I always circumvented the Law when I thought it desirable to do so in the interests of justice." He tells of repeated alibis and prisoners who delighted in escaping, and observes that the habit of nailing culprits by the ear to a post was a useless method of detention, since they preferred to part with their ear rather than their liberty. In chapter four he declares, "I do not think much of juries" and gives several examples where they fouled things up. He notes that "Siamese jails were not very pleasant places" (they were, and perhaps still are, not meant to be) and prisoners "in former times" wore shackles on their feet; by all accounts some things have changed but little. When looking back, in chapter eleven, he declares himself in favour of (non-physical) trial by ordeal, like finding out whose candle of two disputants burns the slowest.

The chapter devoted to marriage tangles includes a man married to a woman with no legs, the exchange of a wife for a buffalo (the buffalo was preferred by both parties since it did not nag) and that cut-off nose. The account of local amusements falls rather flat, apart from the novelty of fighting beetles. There is plenty about ghosts and spirits, including one that inhabited a tree growing by the grave of one Robinson (who is not in the listing of persons interred in the other Wood's *De Mortuis...*, to which volume I must acknowledge thanks for some of the information given here) and nearly caused the death of the person willing to chop it down, but Wood organized a nocturnal mock-exorcism, reciting "The boy stood on the burning deck" with a mock-talisman, and all was well.

Wood does not go gooey over elephants, unlike so many. He probably spent too much time too close to them—the Chiang Mai consulate boasted a few on the payroll in pre-motorized days. He points out how delicate they are, that their memories are not so wonderful, that they develop bad habits, like one consular beast that persisted in disinterring corpses, and that baby elephants, far from being cuddly, "really are an infernal nuisance in every way."

Chapter thirteen is the least successful, with the inappropriate heading "Some exotics". It deals with the hill tribes in a cold factual way, using material acknowledged to come from Gordon Young, and with virtually no personal input. Another tale which does not come off, found in chapter eight, is that concerning the charms supposedly used by Siamese soldiers when showing their skills before Louis XIV; this tall story is lifted from the *Phongsawadan* and acknowledged as such, but is entirely without historical foundation, since no troops ever went to France with the Siamese mini-mission of 1684 or the embassy of 1686.

Wood is on safer ground recalling tales involving mothers-in-law (he hates them), guides who do not know their way, the adaptability of the Siamese and the Lao, and the pitfalls of translations, as with a clerk who turned an invitation marked "Evening dress with decorations" into "Nightdress with ribbons" (machine translations are worse; I was once told of the computerized conversion of "the Bishop of Condom", a pleasant market town in southern France, into "l'évêque des préservatifs", the Bishop of Contraceptives).

The book ends, in chapter fifteen (the chapters are not exactly watertight divisions), appropriately, with a slightly sentimental account of Wood's servant Sing Keo occupying a little bamboo house in his compound, whose wife dies in childbirth, but which nevertheless has a happy ending when he finds a new wife and starts playing his wooden banjo again.

Yes, Wood comes over as an old man with decided personal opinions, but a person of eminent good sense, a slightly wry approach to life, someone very humane, who has seen and mixed with all sorts during his lifetime. This is a very personal work, of undoubted charm. One wishes there were more.

To end on a personal note, I am ashamed to admit that, though I must have met the Grand Old Man of Chiang Mai when on official visits for the British Council there in the early 1960s, I have no recollection of doing do. Other past consular figures remain in mind, though. The tale of the British consular building hardly bears telling. In one of the British government's misguided attempts at penny-pinching, it sold the old building by the river. Then there were legal complications, the details of which are sketchy, and it seems to form part of the compound of a riverside restaurant now, though without being used or repaired. Wood must be turning in his grave (plot D11 in the Chiang Mai Foreign Cemetery on the other side of the river, and with a Wood Memorial close by).

Michael Smithies
Chiang Mai and Bua Yai
3–9 March 2003